ACADEMICS, POLITICS, AND
THE 1972 ELECTION

ACADEMICS, POLITICS, AND THE 1972 ELECTION

Everett Carll Ladd, Jr.
Seymour Martin Lipset

American Enterprise Institute for Public Policy Research
Washington, D. C.

Everett Carll Ladd, Jr., is professor of political science and director of the Social Science Data Center, University of Connecticut. Seymour Martin Lipset is professor of government and sociology, Harvard University.

ISBN 0-8447-3108-0

Domestic Affairs Study 15

Library of Congress Catalog Card No. L. C. 73-86186

Printed in the United States of America

CONTENTS

PREFACE

In the summer of 1972, after the national nominating conventions of both parties had completed their work, and surveys of voter preferences had indicated the continuation of the decisive Republican lead, we became convinced of the desirability of examining the electoral leanings of one relatively small but influential occupational group, the professoriate. For one thing, both of us had been working for some time on the politics of American academics. In particular, we had been engaged in analysis and writing which drew upon a massive national survey of the faculty, conducted in 1969 under the sponsorship of the Carnegie Commission on Higher Education. We have presented details on this survey and our findings in a number of publications.[1] In view of the work already completed, we saw particular merit in the updating which a new 1972 faculty survey would make possible.

The agenda of academic politics had been substantially redrawn between 1969 and 1972. With the war in Vietnam at least the most evident precipitating factor, protests and demonstrations— initiating them, resisting them, trying in some measure to cope with

---

[1] See, among these, "Politics and Polarities—And What Professors Think," *Psychology Today*, vol. 4 (November 1970), pp. 49-51ff; "The Divided Professoriate," *Change*, vol. 3 (May-June 1971), pp. 54-60; "American Social Scientists and the Growth of Campus Political Activism in the 1960's," *Social Science Information*, vol. 10 (April 1971), pp. 105-120; "Jewish Academics in the United States: Their Achievements, Culture and Politics," *American Jewish Year Book* (1971), pp. 89-128; "The Politics of American Political Scientists," *PS*, vol. 4 (Spring 1971), pp. 135-144; "College Generations—From the 1930's to the 1960's," *The Public Interest*, no. 25 (Fall 1971), pp. 99-113; "The Politics of American Sociologists," *American Journal of Sociology*, vol. 78 (July 1972), pp. 67-104; "Politics of Academic Natural Scientists and Engineers," *Science*, vol. 176 (June 1972), pp. 1091-1100.

them—had become in the latter half of the sixties the preoccupation of academics. The literature on universities in this period testifies to the all-absorbing attention to student and faculty political activism. Then, in the early 1970s, higher education entered yet another era, with a new political agenda. "Austerity" in its many forms came to command academic attention as much as protests had earlier. A variety of new issues appeared. A decade ago, for example, unionization of college and university professors appeared unthinkable. Yet in 1972, to a significant degree in response to austerity, the number of faculty and other professional personnel covered by union contracts approached 80,000, and a continuing stream of professorial collective bargaining elections seemed assured.[2] The tone of faculty politics in the sixties was outward looking, preoccupied with concerns over the larger society. By 1972, in contrast, it apparently had become much narrower, more concerned with immediate professional interests and needs. Had professors to some extent become more conservative in a kind of "backlash" from the activism of the sixties and in response to the austerity of the seventies?

There was another reason, very different from the above matter of maintaining continuity in our investigations, for our interest in surveying the politics of professors in 1972, and specifically their commitments in the presidential contest. Along with its base among some depressed minorities, McGovern's strength appeared in the summer of 1972 to rest heavily in the academic-intellectual community. The latter had been, we knew, the major source of the antiwar movement which brought Lyndon Johnson down in 1968, and supplied both the ideological and the activist base for the Kennedy and McCarthy campaigns. How, in fact, was McGovern doing among college professors? Was his strength in the professorial ranks experiencing an erosion comparable to that among other traditionally Democratic groups? Or would professors (along with other segments of the intellectual community) move "against the grain," giving the embattled Democratic nominee perhaps even greater than normal support? How, in general, did academics see the choice between George McGovern and Richard Nixon? What issues moved them most strongly toward, or away from, the incumbent Republican President and his Democratic challenger? To what extent, in short, did the political battleground of 1972, as seen by academics, resemble

[2] We have discussed the unionization of the faculty in *Professors, Unions, and American Higher Education* (Berkeley, Calif.: Carnegie Commission on Higher Education, distributed by McGraw-Hill, 1973).

that on which the presidential contest was being fought out in the larger society?

To deal with these and related matters, we conducted a telephone survey of a national sample of professors in late August and early September, and in November after the election, we again questioned these same respondents through a mailed questionnaire. Our approach was to build these surveys into the structure of the much larger 1969 Carnegie investigation.[3] In the 1969 survey, a disproportionate random sampling design was used to select colleges and universities, in order to obtain adequate numbers of institutions of various types and characteristics. A six in seven random sample of faculty was drawn from the rosters of the included schools, and questionnaires were mailed in March 1969 to 100,315 professors thus chosen for inclusion—nearly one-third of the entire professoriate. In 1972, we assigned all of the four-year colleges and universities included in the 1969 study to a series of categories defined by essential institutional characteristics; then a subset of institutions was randomly selected from each stratum. Rosters of all full-time faculty members at these schools were obtained, from which a random sample was drawn. A ratio was instituted providing that the number selected from a given stratum should constitute the same percentage in the sample as in the entire professoriate.

Between August 29 and September 13, 1972, our staff attempted to interview by telephone each of the 523 academics thus selected for inclusion in the survey. A total of 472 interviews was completed (90 percent). In November 1972, this panel was queried again, using mailed questionnaires, and a response rate of 86 percent was achieved.

Portions of the materials in Chapter 1 first appeared in Lipset's "Academia and Politics in America," in T. J. Nossiter, ed., *Imagination and Precision in the Social Sciences* (London: Faber, 1972), pp. 211-289; and in Lipset's and Richard B. Dobson's "The Intellectual as Critic and Rebel," *Daedalus*, vol. 101 (Summer 1972) pp. 137-198. Chapter 2 was written by Ladd, as part of a larger study of American party coalitions. A fuller treatment of the materials contained in the chapter will be published by W. W. Norton (*The American Party Coalitions: From the New Deal to the Seventies*), as well as in professional journals. We reported briefly on the 1972 faculty survey

---

[3] For comprehensive discussions of the methodology of the 1969 Carnegie survey, see Martin Trow, "Technical Report: Carnegie Commission National Survey of Higher Education," mimeographed (Berkeley: Carnegie Commission on Higher Education, 1972); and Alan Bayer, *College and University Faculty: A Statistical Description*, ACE Research Reports Series, vol. 5, no. 5 (Washington, D. C.: American Council on Education, 1971).

in "Poisoned Ivy: McGovern's Campus Support," *New York*, vol. 5 (October 16, 1972), pages 43-46, which was reprinted with the authors' title ("Contours of Academic Politics: 1972") by the American Enterprise Institute (Reprint No. 6). We are completing a comprehensive study of academic politics in the United States, to be published by McGraw-Hill.

We wish to acknowledge our debt to the American Enterprise Institute which provided financial support for the 1972 surveys, and to the Carnegie Commission on Higher Education which financed the 1969 survey of American academics. We are also indebted to the Guggenheim Foundation for fellowships to each of us and to both the Center for Advanced Study in the Behavioral Sciences at Stanford, California and the Social Science Data Center of the University of Connecticut for support facilities. We are grateful to the Ford Foundation for a grant to Lipset for the study of intellectuals. Finally, we would like to thank Ferdinand Engel and Margaret Pyne for computer-related assistance, Janet Huber, Diane Reed and Anne-Marie Mercure for their help in analyzing the survey data, and Eleanor Wilcox for typing the several drafts of the manuscript with, as usual, expert care. Our special thanks are due Michael Gold who served as study director and ably supervised the collection of the survey data. For the opinions expressed in this volume we must, of course, assume full responsibility.

Everett Carll Ladd, Jr.
Seymour Martin Lipset
May 1973

1
ACADEMICS AND POLITICS
IN THE UNITED STATES

College and university faculty, together with their student apprentices, have established a reputation as one of the most liberal-left strata in the United States—a reputation challenged by few persons at any place on the political spectrum. This proclivity for a politics which is critical of society from the perspectives of liberal and egalitarian values seemingly manifests itself across virtually the entire spectrum of political activity. John Kenneth Galbraith, for instance, has described faculty and students as the fulcrum of the protest politics of the 1960s:

> It was the universities—not the trade unions, nor the freelance intellectuals, nor the press, nor the businessmen . . . —which led the opposition to the Vietnam war, which forced the retirement of President Johnson, which are forcing the pace of our present withdrawal [1971] from Vietnam, which are leading the battle against the great corporations on the issue of pollution, and which at the last congressional elections retired a score or more of the more egregious time-servers, military sycophants and hawks.[1]

Conservatives, while far from sanguine about such a condition, seem generally to concur with Galbraith's assessment. Leading conservative economists such as Friedrich Hayek, Milton Friedman, and George Stigler, had earlier concluded that American university faculty as a group have been a major source of political unrest. Thus, writing in *Newsweek* in 1969, Friedman approvingly cited the comments of his colleague Stigler:

---

[1] John Kenneth Galbraith, "An Adult's Guide to New York, Washington and Other Exotic Places," *New York*, vol. 4 (November 15, 1971), p. 52.

The university is by design and effect the institution and society which creates discontent with the existing moral, social and political institutions and proposes new institutions to replace them. . . . Invited to be learned in the institutions of other times and places, incited to new understandings of the social and physical world, the university faculty is inherently a disruptive force.[2]

Intellectuals as Oppositionists

Such commentary restates in the contemporary context a very old and well-developed theme—that the intellectual community, of which faculty are a part, is inherently questioning, critical, socially disruptive. The great nineteenth century French social commentator, Alexis de Tocqueville, attributed to intellectuals, to the *philosophes,* a potent role in the French Revolution, asserting that they "built up in men's minds an imaginary ideal society in which all was simple, uniform, coherent, equitable, and rational in the full sense of the term. It was this vision of the perfect State that fired the imagination of the masses and little by little estranged them from the here-and-now."[3] Later, in a study of the 1848 revolutionary eruption, the English historian Lewis Namier described it as "primarily the revolution of the intellectuals—*la révolution des clercs.*" He saw the 1848 events as the "outcome of thirty-three creative years," in which intellectuals across Europe fostered, in Lamartine's words, "a moral idea, of reason, logic, sentiment . . . a desire . . . for a better order of government and society."[4] Raymond Aron has written generally of "the tendency to criticize the established order [as], so to speak, the occupational disease of the intellectuals."[5]

In the United States nearly a century ago, Whitelaw Reid, abolitionist leader and then editor of the *New York Tribune,* delivered a series of commencement addresses dealing with the subject of "The Scholar in Politics" in which he argued that

exceptional influences eliminated, the scholar is pretty sure to be opposed to the established. The universities of Ger-

---

[2] George Stigler, unpublished memorandum as cited by Milton Friedman, "The Ivory Tower," *Newsweek,* vol. 74 (November 10, 1969), p. 92.

[3] Alexis de Tocqueville, *The Old Regime and the French Revolution* (Garden City, N. Y.: Doubleday Anchor Books, 1955), pp. 146-147.

[4] Lewis Namier, *1848: The Revolution of the Intellectuals* (Garden City, N. Y.: Doubleday Anchor Books, 1964), p. 2.

[5] Raymond Aron, *The Opium of the Intellectuals* (New York: W. W. Norton & Co., Inc., 1962), p. 210.

many contain the deadliest foes to the absolute authority of the Kaiser. The scholars of France prepared the way for the first Revolution, and were the most dangerous enemies of the imperial adventurer who betrayed the second. . . . While the prevailing parties in our country [the United States] were progressive and radical, the temper of our colleges was to the last degree conservative. As our politics settled into the conservative tack, a fresh wind began to blow about the college seats, and literary men, at last furnished inspiration for the splendid movement that swept slavery from the statute book. . . . Wise unrest will always be their [the scholars'] chief trait. We may set down . . . the very foremost function of the scholar in politics, *to oppose the established.*[6]

In our period, Daniel Patrick Moynihan observed (in a pre-inauguration memorandum to President Nixon advising him what to expect), that since "about 1840, the cultural elite have pretty generally rejected the values and activities of the larger society. It has been said of America that the culture [intellectual elite] will not approve that which the polity strives to provide."[7]

The argument, then, is that the intellectual role—in which academics partake to varying degrees—predisposes toward a critical, questioning, oppositionist political stance, to what Lionel Trilling insightfully described as the "adversary culture."[8]

What is it about intellectuality which so frequently leads those associated with this role component to be oppositionists? Some of the literature on intellectuals has avoided the question by assuming the word intellectual to apply only to educated and culturally creative people who are consciously at odds with the social system in which they dwell. But as Carmichael points out, to define the category as comprising only those who have "in common a certain sociopolitical

---

[6] Whitelaw Reid, "The Scholar in Politics," *Scribner's Monthly,* vol. 6 (1873), pp. 613-614. Reid first made these observations in commencement addresses delivered at Dartmouth and at Amherst, and in remarks before the alumni of Miami University. (Emphasis in the original.) Twenty-eight years later, speaking at Stanford University, an older Reid saw the same behavior by American academics as deplorable. "It is a misfortune for the colleges, and no less for the country, when the trusted instructors are out of sympathy with its history, with its development, and with the men who made the one and are guiding the other." Reid, *American and English Studies,* vol. 1 (New York: Scribner's, 1913), pp. 214-242.

[7] As printed in the *New York Times,* March 11, 1970.

[8] Lionel Trilling, *Beyond Culture* (New York: Viking Press, 1965), pp. xii-xiii.

radicalism" makes for tautology if the question at hand is the source of the politics of the intellectuals.[9]

The most satisfactory approach, we think, is to begin as Hofstadter did, with the distinction between "intellect" and "intelligence."

> Intellect . . . is the critical, creative, and contemplative side of mind. . . . Intellect evaluates evaluations, and looks for meanings of situations as a whole. . . . Intelligence is an excellence of mind that is employed within a fairly narrow, immediate, and predictable range; it is a manipulative, adjustive, unfailing practical quality. . . . Intelligence works within the framework of limited but clearly stated goals. . . .[10]

As such, intelligence is presumably common to people in all occupations; whereas intellectuality is far less frequently encountered. There are very few intellectuals who spend their entire vocational energies on efforts at creation or innovation, but it is some "critical mass" of this commitment which defines the intellectual.

The capacity for criticism, for rejection of the status quo, is not simply a matter of preference by some intellectuals for this attitude of mind, if the above distinction is accepted. The intellectual's activities involve the creation of new knowledge, new ideas, new art. Reality is held up to the test of the ideal, the theoretic. Various observers of intellectual life have pointed to the ways in which emphasis on critical work and creativity within specific fields often has led the more original to formulate general critiques of society. Thus, Joseph Schumpeter called attention to the fact that the "humanists [of the Renaissance] were primarily philologists but . . . they quickly expanded into the fields of manners, politics, religion and philosophy . . . from criticism of a text to criticism of a society, the way is shorter than it seems."[11]

Finally, understanding of the critical orientation of intellectuals requires attention to the creation of a new social role in response to the massive social changes of the last two and a half centuries. This subject is far too large to be handled adequately in the present work, but some brief attention is essential.[12] A set of social and economic

---

[9] Joel Carmichael, *A Short History of the Russian Revolution* (New York: Basic Books, 1964), p. 223.

[10] Richard Hofstadter, *Anti-Intellectualism in American Life* (New York: Vintage Books, 1962), p. 25.

[11] Joseph Schumpeter, *Capitalism, Socialism and Democracy* (New York: Harper Torchbooks, 1962), p. 148.

[12] Ladd has dealt with this subject at some length in *Ideology in America: Change and Response in a City, a Suburb, and a Small Town* (New York: W. W. Norton & Co., 1972), pp. 17-52; and in *American Political Parties: Social Change and Political Response* (New York: W. W. Norton & Co., 1970), pp. 15-27.

transformations began in the seventeenth and eighteenth centuries in Western Europe, the various dimensions of which have received different names: industrial, if we look at economic life; scientific and technological, if attention is drawn to the explosion of knowledge; egalitarian, if the focus is on participation or involvement in the making of decisions for the system, the overturning of societies based upon the aristocratic principle. Ascriptive class societies have not been rare historically. In their various forms, in fact, they represent the principal variety of post-primitive social organization. Egalitarian societies are historically exceptional. The massive repudiation of aristocratic arrangements after the seventeenth century in Western Europe and, since then, throughout the world is among the handful of fundamental political events.

What occurred was, that with the transition from agricultural to industrial systems, resources enormously expanded. Only when there is no possibility of most men living beyond bare subsistence, no matter what the manner of distribution, is it possible that the millions will readily acquiesce to exceptional privileges for the few, from which they and their children are formally and permanently excluded. In societies of gross scarcity, if any culture is to flourish, it is only through the arbitrary extension of privilege to a few. Aristocracy offers a morally tenable standard for parceling scarce values only in scarcity-bound societies. Let the pie dramatically expand— and that is what the economic-technological developments began to achieve in the seventeenth and eighteenth centuries—and groups of men outside the hereditary privileged class will come forward to claim their share, will come to believe that life owes them something more than perpetual wretchedness.

These egalitarian-industrial-technological changes can properly be described as a revolution, and from its beginnings in seventeenth-century Europe this revolution has progressed through a number of stages and has pushed out to become global. From our perspective here, the most important feature of this massive revolutionary surge is that major change became a constant. All manner of social and political institutions were forced into a process of continuing adaptation. In this context, the need arose for a category of people who could explain and chart and direct the flow of societal response, "to help society adjust to novel conditions while discarding outmoded patterns."[13] The historian Carl Becker has nicely described the emergence of this new social role:

---

[13] The quotation is from Paul F. Lazarsfeld and Wagner Thielens, Jr., *The Academic Mind* (Glencoe, Ill.: The Free Press, 1958), p. 151.

Until recently the chief function of the sophisticated, the priests and scribes, has been to stabilize custom and validate social authority by perpetuating the tradition and interpreting it in a manner conformable to the understanding of common man. During the last three hundred years . . . there has emerged a new class of learned men, successors to the priests and scribes, whose function is to increase rather than to preserve knowledge, to undermine rather than to stabilize custom and social authority.[14]

The Disproportionate Liberalism of American Academics

That the pressure "to undermine rather than to stabilize custom and social authority" is compatible with a conservative or right-wing position, as well as with a liberal or radical stance, has been amply demonstrated in our own century. In Europe, intellectual opposition to the status quo in the years after World War I was often represented by right-wing extremist criticism of democracy for creating a mass society in which the vulgar tastes of the populous were seen destroying creative culture, or in which populist demigods undermined national values. This position was found particularly among Catholic intellectuals, and in significant segments of the German academic world. It helped to undermine support for democracy in a number of countries. Wilhelm Ropke, for example, observed that

> in Germany . . . where the university professor has always had exceptional standing . . . it was from the universities that most of the other intellectuals drew the disintegrating poison that they distributed. . . . Naturally the faculties of social science provided a special opportunity for practicing intellectual treachery and preparing the way for Nazism. . . . It is mainly the names of jurists and philosophers that could here be given.[15]

The lead given by German professors was followed by their students. The Nazi student movement captured most of the universities by 1931, winning control of the national student organization and dominating student council elections, before the Nazis won over any other segment of German life. This followed the lead set earlier by

[14] Carl Becker, *Progress and Power* (Stanford: Stanford University Press, 1936), p. 93.

[15] Wilhelm Ropke, "National Socialism and Intellectuals," in George B. de Huszar, ed., *The Intellectuals* (New York: The Free Press, 1960), pp. 346-348.

Italian students, who constituted one of the earliest major sources of Fascist strength there before Mussolini won absolute power.[16]

In this same period, antibourgeois, elitist, or overtly antidemocratic sentiments led a small minority of leading American professors and other intellectuals to find reason to praise Italian fascism. Among the prominent Americans who wrote favorably of fascism were writers such as Wallace Stevens and Henry Miller, a variety of humanistic scholars, including Irving Babbitt, Charles Beard, Shepard Clough, Carlton J. H. Hayes, Horace Kallen, William Lyon Phelps, George Santayana, and Herbert Schneider.

However, the record seems to validate Richard Hofstadter's generalization that throughout the twentieth century the political weight of American academics and other intellectuals has been committed to the progressive, liberal or leftist side.[17] This bias reflects in considerable measure the weakness of a legitimate national conservative tradition in the United States, since the ideology of Americanism, based on principles enunciated in the Declaration of Independence, itself emphasizes the values of egalitarianism and populism. Thus, when American intellectuals have become aware of the gap between the ideal and the reality, between what is and what was (in a bygone Jeffersonian utopia of equal yeomen farmers) or what should be (a classless participatory future), they have challenged the system for not fulfilling ideals inherent in the American creed.[18]

There is by now an impressive body of empirical data demonstrating that the politics of American academics, for at least the last half century, have been disproportionately left of center.[19] From the 1930s on, for example, there are varieties of data dealing with party and candidate choice which reveal the relative liberalism of college professors, in decisive fashion when compared to other segments of the middle class, but also in comparison with manual workers and low-income groups generally. In 1937, a Chicago survey reported pro-New Deal sentiments among 84 percent of professors

[16] Guido Martinotti, "A Positive Marginality: Notes on Students and Periods of Political Mobilization," in Lipset and Philip Altbach, eds., *Students in Revolt* (Boston: Houghton-Mifflin Co., 1969), pp. 173-174.

[17] Hofstadter, *Anti-Intellectualism in American Life*, p. 39.

[18] Lipset has discussed these themes in *The First New Nation: The United States in Historical and Comparative Perspective* (Garden City, N. Y.: Doubleday Anchor Books, 1967); and in *Revolution and Counterrevolution* (Garden City, N. Y.: Doubleday Anchor Books, 1970).

[19] For a discussion of various studies bearing on this point, see Lipset, *Political Man* (Garden City, N. Y.: Doubleday Anchor Books, 1963), pp. 332-371; and "Academia and Politics in America," in T. J. Nossiter, ed., *Imagination and Precision in the Social Sciences* (London: Faber, 1972), pp. 211-289.

of social science and 65 percent of natural science faculty members, as contrasted with 56 percent among manual workers, and only about 15 percent in the ranks of lawyers, physicians, dentists, and engineers.[20] A 1947 survey of 9,000 university graduates indicated large Democratic majorities in the 1944 election among teachers, scientists, and people in the arts. It is interesting that while 60 percent of those who reported their occupation as "scientists" voted for Franklin Roosevelt, 80 percent of those who listed themselves as engineers opted for his Republican opponent, Thomas Dewey.[21] A questionnaire administered to 1,300 professors in fifteen colleges and universities in October 1956 revealed disproportionate backing for the Democratic and leftist third party candidates in the 1948 and 1952 elections, and a heavy Democratic preference in 1956 vote intent. Harry Truman received 50 percent of faculty votes in 1948, while Progressive party candidate Henry Wallace and Socialist Norman Thomas took about 10 percent.[22] (The Democratic and left third party candidates were backed by just over 50 percent of all voters, about 10 percent less than in the academic community.) Dwight Eisenhower swept the country in 1952 with 55 percent of the vote, but Adlai Stevenson was supported by 54 percent of academics. Various third parties on the left garnered just over 2 percent of the academic vote. In 1956, Stevenson's backing among professors rose to 60 percent.[23]

The voting behavior of academic social scientists in the postwar elections was examined in a survey conducted by Paul F. Lazarsfeld and Wagner Thielens, Jr. in 1955. Although confined to a single discipline group—and that known to be the most liberal and Democratic within the faculty—the Lazarsfeld-Thielens investigation is nonetheless especially interesting because it is the first national survey of the politics of academics to apply fully the methods of systematic sampling. Lazarsfeld and Thielens found that 63 percent of social scientists voted for Harry Truman in 1948, 8 percent for Henry Wallace or Norman Thomas, and only 28 percent for Republican Thomas Dewey. Four years later, Stevenson took 65 percent of the social scientists' vote, as contrasted with 34 percent for Eisenhower.[24]

[20] Arthur Kornhauser, "Attitudes of Economic Groups," *Public Opinion Quarterly*, vol. 2 (1938), p. 264.

[21] *Time College Graduate Study, 1947*; data made available through the Roper Public Opinion Research Center, Williamstown, Massachusetts.

[22] Lawrence C. Howard, "The Academic and the Ballot," *School and Society*, vol. 86 (November 22, 1958), pp. 415-419.

[23] Ibid.

[24] Lazarsfeld and Thielens, *The Academic Mind*, p. 402.

Table 1

PRESIDENTIAL PREFERENCES OF FACULTY, THE ELECTORATE AT LARGE, AND SELECTED POPULATION SUBGROUPS 1964 AND 1968

(all data presented as row percentages)

	1964			1968			
	Dem.	Rep.	Other	Dem.	Rep.	AIP	Other
Faculty [a]	77	22	1	58	38	1	3
U.S. electorate	61.1	38.5	.4	42.7	43.4	13.5	.2
Manual workers [b]	71	29	c	50	35	15	c
Members of labor union families	73	27	c	56	29	15	c
Professionals and business managers [b]	54	46	c	34	56	10	c
Grade school educated [b]	66	34	c	52	33	15	c
High school educated [b]	62	38	c	42	43	15	c
College educated [b]	52	48	c	37	54	9	c

[a] Data from 1969 Carnegie faculty survey.

[b] Data from Gallup survey data, as reported in the *Gallup Opinion Index*, Report No. 90 (December 1972), p. 10.

[c] Less than one percent.

As far as we know, there was no national survey of faculty choice in the 1960 election, but the big Carnegie national survey conducted at the end of the sixties provides unusually comprehensive data on the 1964 and 1968 presidential preferences of professors, along with other aspects of their political orientations. Lyndon Johnson was backed by 77 percent of professors, in contrast to 52 percent of the college-educated population generally and 54 percent of persons in professional and managerial occupations (Table 1). The faculty was then 20 to 25 percentage points more Democratic than groups of comparable social economic status in the population at large. In fact, academics gave Johnson a higher proportion of their votes than any other distinguishable occupational or class stratum. The relative distributions in the 1968 contest between Hubert Humphrey and Richard Nixon were essentially the same. Fifty-eight percent of professors voted for Humphrey, according to the Carnegie survey, in comparison to 43 percent of the electorate, 50 percent of manual workers, and just 37 percent of the college educated.

Survey data bearing on the relative liberalism of American college professors are not limited to electoral behavior. We know that academics turned against the war in Vietnam earlier than other groups in the population. A national survey of professors conducted by the National Opinion Research Center (NORC) in 1966 found just over half (51 percent) opposed to the government's Vietnam policies, the large majority from "dovish" perspectives.[25] At the time this study was being conducted, Gallup reported that only about a third of the general public considered American intervention in Vietnam to be a mistake.[26] Not until the summer of 1968 did a majority of those interviewed indicate that they considered the intervention wrong.[27]

College faculty continued their record of opposition to the war. In the Carnegie survey, taken in the spring of 1969, a majority (60 percent) favored getting out, either by withdrawing all American troops immediately (19 percent) or by encouraging "the emergence of a coalition government in South Vietnam" (41 percent). Only two-fifths of professors supported the emerging policy of "Vietnamization" or backed an even greater military effort: 33 percent maintained that "the U.S. should try to reduce its involvement, while being sure to prevent a Communist takeover in the South," while 7 percent favored committing "whatever forces are necessary to defeat the Communists." An almost identical question on Vietnam was presented to the general public through a Gallup survey eight months later, in December 1969. Fifty-six percent of those interviewed endorsed either Vietnamization or "more military force," alternatives which were backed by only 40 percent of the professoriate in the preceding spring.[28]

Similar evidence concerning the greater liberalism of college faculty as compared to the public at large, and to other occupational groups, high and low, well educated or not, may be adduced for a

---

[25] See Edward Noll and Peter H. Rossi, "General Social and Economic Attitudes of College and University Faculty Members," mimeographed (Chicago: National Opinion Research Center, 1966), p. 53.

[26] The Gallup Poll: Public Opinion 1935-1971, vol. 3 (New York: Random House, 1972), p. 2031.

[27] Hazel Erskine, "The Polls: Is War a Mistake?" Public Opinion Quarterly, vol. 34 (Spring 1970), p. 134.

[28] The Gallup Poll, vol. 3, p. 232. In this Gallup survey, conducted between December 12 and December 15 of 1969, the "Vietnamization" alternative was phrased as "withdraw troops but take as many years to do this as are needed to turn the war over to the South Vietnamese"; while the "more force" choice was framed as "send more troops to Vietnam and step up the fighting." The former was endorsed by 44 percent of the population, the latter by 12 percent.

variety of other issues ranging from the rights of black Americans to legalization of marijuana. Close to half (45 percent) of the white faculty interviewed in the Carnegie survey agreed with the statement that "the main cause of Negro riots in the cities is white racism." Only 20 percent strongly disagreed with this interpretation. In contrast, a Gallup survey of the general public in May 1968 found that 73 percent of whites believed that in their community Negroes are treated "the same as whites are," a position taken by 54 percent who had attended college. Over half (54 percent) of those interviewed by Gallup in this survey also said that "Negroes themselves . . . [are] more to blame for the present conditions in which Negroes find themselves . . . [than] white people." [29] The faculty also appears significantly more liberal on an issue which touches an especially raw nerve in contemporary American politics—school busing to achieve racial integration. A Gallup survey conducted in March 1970 found that only 14 percent of the public favored "the busing of Negro and white children" on behalf of integration, while 81 percent were opposed. Just 11 percent of whites, and 13 percent of the college educated, endorsed the proposal.[30] A Harris survey conducted in the same month found a similar distribution. Only 19 percent of the public favored busing for integration, even if "it could be worked out so that there was no more busing of school children than there is now," whereas 73 percent were opposed and 8 percent unsure.[31] Among respondents to the 1969 Carnegie survey, however, 46 percent supported busing to achieve "racial integration of the public schools," with 54 percent opposed.

Faculty, along with college students, are also much more inclined than the general public to describe their politics as left of center (Table 2). Forty-five percent of undergraduates, and 42 percent of graduate students, identified their political leanings as "left" or "liberal" in companion surveys sponsored by the Carnegie Commission at about the same time as the faculty study was being conducted. Forty-six percent of their professors located their own politics on the liberal-left end of the scale. By way of contrast, a 1970 Gallup survey found only a fifth of the general public describing themselves as "very liberal" or "fairly liberal."

[29] Hazel Erskine, "The Polls: Recent Opinion on Racial Problems," *Public Opinion Quarterly*, vol. 32 (Winter 1968-1969), pp. 669-670.

[30] *Gallup Opinion Index*, Report No. 58 (April 1970), p. 9.

[31] *The Harris Survey Yearbook, 1970* (New York: Louis Harris and Associates, 1971), p. 229.

Table 2

POLITICAL IDEOLOGY OF ACADEMICS AND GENERAL PUBLIC IN THE UNITED STATES

(all data presented as row percentages)

Political Ideology	Under-graduates [a]	Graduate Students [a]	Faculty [a]	U.S. Public [b]
Left	5	5	5	4
Liberal	40	37	41	16
Middle-of-the-road	36	28	27	38
Moderately conservative	17	26	25	32
Strongly conservative	2	4	3	10

[a] Response to the question "How would you characterize yourself politically at the present time (left, liberal, middle-of-the-road, moderately conservative, or strongly conservative)?" Data from 1969 Carnegie Commission surveys.

[b] Response to the question "How would you describe yourself (very liberal, fairly liberal, middle-of-the-road, fairly conservative, or very conservative)?" Data from Gallup Opinion Index, Report No. 65 (November 1970), p. 17.

Some who recognize that professors are more inclined than other groups to favor liberal, and even radical, social change argue, nonetheless, that such support ends at the borders of the campus, that faculty are "conservative" with respect to the university. Clark Kerr was making this point when he wrote that "few institutions are so conservative as universities about their own affairs while their members are so liberal about the affairs of others. . . ." [32] This observation has considerable validity. Many academics who are liberal or left on larger social issues have proved relatively conservative in their reactions to campus events, particularly in recent years on issues stemming from student demonstrations, and demands that they share "power" with students. Yet insofar as it has been possible to compare the attitudes of professors on such matters with those of the public at large, once again the former appear more supportive of what might be described as the liberal or "permissive" positions.

At the outset, it may be noted that the faculty and the general public reacted in sharply different ways to what was perhaps the most salient event of the 1960s in which campus-based activism affected the larger political process—the demonstrations and riots that occurred during the 1968 Democratic Convention in Chicago. Three-fifths (59 percent) of professors included in the Carnegie

[32] Clark Kerr, *The Uses of the University* (New York: Harper Torchbooks, 1966), p. 99.

survey disagreed with the statement that the "police acted reasonably in curbing the demonstrations at the Democratic Convention." When a comparable question was asked of the national sample by the Survey Research Center of the University of Michigan (SRC) only 25 percent indicated they thought the police had "used too much force" in dealing with the Chicago demonstrators. Responses to this question varied significantly with education, and the highly educated were more likely to be critical of the police actions. Even so, only 37 percent of college graduates and 52 percent of those with graduate degrees—compared to 59 percent of professors—were generally critical of the Chicago police.[33] Interestingly, only 36 percent in the general public who supported Eugene McCarthy for the Democratic nomination believed that police had been over zealous. Even those under thirty who supported the antiwar candidate were evenly divided, with 50 percent claiming that "too much force" had been used.

American faculty members were both ambivalent and sharply divided in their reaction to the campus activism of the late 1960s. In 1969, 42 percent stated that they approved "of the emergence of radical student activism in recent years," while 58 percent disapproved. It is clear from their answers to a variety of questions in the Carnegie survey that most professors were bothered by the recourse in some demonstrations to illegal methods, particularly the seizure of buildings and efforts to prevent classes from being held. A substantial majority, 77 percent, felt in 1969 that "students who disrupted the functioning of a college should be expelled or suspended." But at the same time, only one quarter of the professors queried thought that student demonstrations "have no place on a college campus."

No precisely comparable questions have been asked of the public. National polls taken during the era of frequent student demonstrations, however, suggest overwhelming public hostility. Thus, in the spring of 1969, 94 percent of respondents in a Gallup sample said that they would "like to see college administrators take a stronger stand on student disorders."[34] A year later, during the wave of protests which swept through university circles against the Cambodian incursion, 82 percent expressed opposition to "college students going on strike to protest the way things are run in our country."[35] When asked during the Cambodian events to list the

---

[33] John Robinson, "Public Reaction to Political Protest: Chicago 1968," *Public Opinion Quarterly*, vol. 34 (Spring 1970), p. 7.

[34] *Gallup Opinion Index*, Report No. 49 (July 1969), p. 26.

[35] *The Gallup Poll*, vol. 3, p. 2250.

most important problem facing the country, the public put "campus unrest" at the head of the list.[36]

Proposals to make universities more democratic by involving students in various institutional decisions were offered as an accompaniment to the political unrest of the 1960s. For the most part, such proposals called for students sharing power with the faculty in decisions about curriculum, admissions policy, discipline, and academic appointments. When queried about such matters in the 1969 Carnegie survey, professors were most resistant to the last: a majority (55 percent) thought that students should have "little or no role" in evaluating faculty for appointment and promotion. Even here, however, it may be argued that with almost half endorsing some student involvement in faculty hiring and firing, there is testimony to considerable professorial "liberalism" with regard to "their own turf." Large, although varying, majorities of professors favored students taking part in decisions concerning the "provision and content of courses," "undergraduate admissions policy," "bachelor's degree requirements," and "student discipline."

Again, it is difficult to find precisely similar questions addressed by pollsters to the general public. But two Gallup surveys come close. In December 1968, Gallup asked a national sample whether they thought "students should or should not have a greater say concerning the academic side of the college—that is the courses, examinations, and so forth?" Only one-third replied that they should. Among those who had been to college, the level of support rose to 39 percent, but 58 percent of this group opposed any further student involvement.[37] Four months later, Gallup inquired whether "you think college students should or should not have a greater say in the running of colleges." Support for a "greater say," put in general terms, was even less than in the preceding poll, only 17 percent. It would seem clear from these data that the "upper class" of the university has been more "liberal" with respect to proposed limitations on their intramural authority than has the public at large.

Class, Intellectuality, and Faculty Politics

In examining a variety of studies of American academics extending back over the last half century, we have encountered a seeming paradox: that the "top" of the academic community is more liberal

---

[36] Ibid., p. 2252.
[37] Ibid., p. 2178.

or left of center than the "bottom." That is, in a group whose disproportionate liberalism has been well established, the more successful, highly achieving and amply rewarded members display the greatest inclination to support politics of social criticism from perspectives of egalitarian and popular values. The leading figures in universities stand to the left of the "backbenchers," of the rank and file.

This appears at first glance a paradox, in large part because of our intellectual readiness to apply "the class theory of politics." This theory—perhaps better described as a set of assumptions—holds that tendencies to criticize society are related to objective deprivation and discrimination, that a politics of change finds its natural supporters among those who suffer from the status quo, that being well rewarded and recognized makes for conservatism just as being deprived produces liberal and egalitarian perspectives. The application of the class theory of politics to the university world carries with it the argument that those who consult for business and government, receive large research grants, hold tenured and high-salaried positions at major universities, publish extensively, and dominate the professional activities of their discipline have thus been co-opted into "the system." The argument supposes that they have the most to lose from any significant social or academic change and must be the most conservative members of the professoriate.

Clearly, application of what we have called the "class theory" helps account for a good many features of contemporary political behavior, and there has been a tendency, especially in recent years, for left critics throughout the university to carry it over largely unmodified into an explanation of professorial politics. For example, Professor Noam Chomsky has decried the role of academic social science in contributing to the ideas and values of the "new mandarins" who guided American involvement in Vietnam, and he attributed to the "dominants" of the profession the most conservative or apologist mentality. "In general" Chomsky wrote,

> one would expect any group with access to power and affluence to construct an ideology that will justify this state of affairs on grounds of the general welfare. For just this reason, Bell's thesis that intellectuals are moving closer to the center of power . . . is to some extent supported by the phenomenon of counterrevolutionary subordination noted earlier. That is, one might anticipate that as power becomes more accessible, the inequities of the society will recede from vision, the status quo will seem less flawed, and the

preservation of order will become a matter of transcendent importance.[38]

The radical caucuses which formed in the latter half of the 1960s, especially in the social sciences but also in the humanities and natural sciences, have devoted considerable attention to what they perceive as the conservatism of their respective "establishments." Alan Wolfe argued that professionalism and professional achievement in political science have been associated with "an affiliation with client-groups which are supportive of existing American policies," and with "support [for] the contemporary American status quo."[39] A pamphlet composed by a group of literature professors contended that the conservative emphasis in their disciplines was determined by a small elite located in the major universities. They objected to the profession's emphasis on "notions of professional integrity, pure scholarship and academic integrity."[40]

The identification of research and scholarly achievement with careerism and support for established policies went so far that one scholar could publish an article, "Is Research Counterrevolutionary?" and answer his rhetorical question with a definite yes. Burt Meyers maintained that "the scientist's research may well be not merely split off from his political activism but actually at odds with it." He contended that even most "pure" scientific research inevitably can and will be misused.

> For example, while bright microbiologists decode the DNA and RNA molecules, hack technicians apply their findings to breed mutant strains of virulent microbes resistant to treatment and capable of incorporation in aerosols for germ warfare. Similar applications have been made or are planned (or can be anticipated by anyone familiar with the dynamics of technology) for findings in the physics of optics, in psychopharmacology, in the social psychology of attitude change, in ecology, in fact, in virtually all branches of science.[41]

---

[38] Noam Chomsky, *American Power and the New Mandarins* (New York: Pantheon Books, 1969), pp. 27-28.

[39] Alan Wolfe, "The Professional Mystique," in Marvin Surkin and Alan Wolfe, eds., *An End to Political Science: The Caucus Papers* (New York: Basic Books, 1970), p. 299.

[40] Ellen Cantarow, with help from Jim Goldberg, Louis Kampf, Katherine Kremen, and the Radical Caucus, *The Great Training Robbery* (Chicago: New University Conference, n.d.), pp. 7-8.

[41] Burt Meyers, "Is Research Counterrevolutionary?" *The Radical Teacher* (Chicago: New University Conference, n.d.), pp. 10-11.

In short, those applying the class theory of politics to universities have pictured the most highly achieving and successful—by current discipline standards—as having the most to lose from any significant change, either in the university or in the larger society, and hence likely to be the most supportive of the status quo. Contact with the federal government (receipt of grants, work as a consultant, et cetera) is especially conducive to conservative attitudes. Challenge to the conservative academic establishment comes, as it must, from the "backbenchers," especially younger members who reject professionalism.

There is, however, an alternative model applicable to academic politics which leads to very different assumptions about the political orientations of "dominants" and "backbenchers." As we have noted, an extensive literature spanning several centuries has stressed the general tendency of achieving intellectuals to support a politics of social criticism. If the natural posture of the intellectual is that of critic, and currently that of the intellectual in the United States to criticize from a liberal-left perspective, then the most intellectually achieving among academics might be expected to display relatively more left-of-center commitments.

How does one go about assessing and measuring intellectuality when dealing with a population group like the professorial community? The assumption that the most intellectual members of the faculty are likely to be the most socially critical is a hard one to test decisively. However, there seem to be ample grounds, from both sense impressions and systematic studies, for maintaining that academic achievement is a good general indicator of intellectual bent. That surely is what universities are supposed to be about. Success in securing a position at a major institution, a high level of scholarly publications, the ability to acquire research support, and general recognition from one's colleagues are indicators of scholarly achievement and reward. They provide the best measures of intellectuality we can expect to attain for large collections of faculty, where we were required to work with objective information, and they seem broadly satisfactory. These characteristics, of course, identify the "dominants" in the universities.

At this point, we should review briefly some other extant data demonstrating the disproportionate liberalism of high achievers among American academics, in comparison to the rank and file. The earliest studies of faculty attitudes—analyses of variation in religious beliefs conducted by James Leuba, a psychologist, in 1913-14 and again in 1933—revealed that the more distinguished professors, both among natural and social scientists, were much more irreligious than their less eminent colleagues.[42] Leuba found, furthermore, that the higher the standard of eminence or achievement, the greater the degree of disbelief. For example, he asked his panel of expert evaluators in sociology to break the "greater" group into two parts, eminent and most eminent. In 1933, 20 percent of the former were believers, but only 5 percent of the latter. Although religious and political beliefs are clearly quite different, many investigations have shown significant intercorrelation: religious unbelief, in the sense that Leuba was defining it, in terms of adherence to conventional religious doctrine, has been associated with liberal political values among Americans.

In the mid-1950s Lazarsfeld and Thielens found a clear relationship between the scholarly achievement of social scientists and propensity for a more liberal-left attitude on the one hand, and more activist politics on the other. For example, highly published social scientists showed up more supportive of civil liberties than colleagues who had not published at all. Professors who had published, who had been officers of professional associations, and who had served as consultants, gave more backing to liberal nominees in 1948 and 1952 presidential elections than did their less highly achieving colleagues. By all measures of academic standing or attainment, the "dominant" social scientists of the McCarthy era proved more inclined to an activist political style and showed greater willingness to defend controversial positions publicly.[43]

The findings of such previous investigations received impressive confirmation from our own 1969 Carnegie survey of academics. The more scholarly and highly achieving faculty appear significantly more disposed to liberal-left views than the entire professoriate.[44] Table 3 shows, for example, that 74 percent of faculty at "elite" colleges and universities favored, in 1969, either an immediate unilateral with-

---

[42] James H. Leuba, *The Belief in God and Immortality* (Chicago: Open Court Publishing Co., 1921), pp. 219-237; and *The Reformation of the Churches* (Boston: The Beacon Press, 1950), pp. 50-54. For a summary article see James Leuba, "Religious Beliefs of American Scientists," *Harpers*, vol. 169 (August 1934), pp. 291-300.

[43] Raw data from the Lazarsfeld-Thielens survey of social scientists were made available to us by the Bureau of Applied Social Research of Columbia University. Further tabulations from these data bearing on the point discussed here have been presented by us in "The Politics of American Sociologists," pp. 81-82.

[44] We have discussed this subject and presented various data bearing upon it in other publications. See "The Divided Professoriate," ". . . And What Professors Think," "The Politics of American Social Scientists," "Politics of Academic Natural Scientists and Engineers," and "The Politics of American Sociologists" (Preface, Footnote 1).

Table 3

POLITICAL ORIENTATIONS OF ACADEMICS, BY SCHOLARLY STANDING AND ACHIEVEMENT; 1969 CARNEGIE FACULTY SURVEY

(all data presented as percentages of n)

	Support Busing For Integration[a]	Support Immediate U.S. Withdrawal from Vietnam or Coalition Government With Viet Cong[b]	1964 Vote for Johnson	1968 Vote		Support "Radical Student Activism"[c]	Very Liberal and Liberal (Liberalism-Conservatism Scale)
				For Humphrey	For left third party		
All faculty (n=60,028)	46	59	78	58	2	43	39
School quality							
1. Elite (n=19,089)	55	74	87	71	3	50	55
2. Middle tier (n=30,042)	45	61	78	59	2	44	40
3. Lowest tier (n=10,872)	42	51	73	52	2	38	31
Consultants-Grantees (n=3,570)	52	70	88	70	2	46	50
High Achievers (n=4,668)	54	76	89	71	3	48	55
Low Achievers (n=9,132)	41	50	73	52	2	38	31

a "Racial integration of the public elementary schools should be achieved even if it requires busing." [Strongly agree, agree with reservations; disagree with reservations; strongly disagree]

b "Which of these positions on Vietnam is closest to your own?" [The U.S. should withdraw from Vietnam immediately; the U.S. should reduce its involvement and encourage the emergence of a coalition government in South Vietnam; the U.S. should try to reduce its involvement, while being sure to prevent a Communist takeover in the South; the U.S. should commit whatever forces are necessary to defeat the Communists]

c "What do you think of the emergence of radical student activism in recent years?" [Unreservedly approve; approve with reservations; disapprove with reservations; unreservedly disapprove]

drawal of American troops from Vietnam or a reduction of involvement coupled with support for a coalition government including the Viet Cong; these positions were taken by only 51 percent of faculty at schools of the lowest tier.[45] Hubert Humphrey received the votes of 71 percent of "elite" school professors in 1968, but only 52 percent support at schools of the lowest range. Fifty-five percent of academics at "elite" institutions were located in the two most liberal categories of a five-item liberalism-conservatism scale, in comparison to 40 percent of their colleagues at middle-tier institutions and just 31 percent of those at schools of the lowest tier.[46]

In comparing the orientations of the most successful and influential academics to the general membership of the profession, we worked with a number of other vehicles for defining the former. One of these comprised "high achievers"—faculty who have gained positions at major universities ("elite" schools as described in note 45) and have also maintained a high level of scholarly productivity (five or more professional publications in the two years preceding the survey). "Low achievers," in contrast, are faculty at institutions of the lowest quality standing who have contributed little to active scholarship (two publications or less in the preceding twenty-four months). We see in Table 3 a marked contrast between these two groups of faculty in all political measures, with the "high achievers" consistently to the left. For instance, 68 percent of those with high academic attainment, contrasted to just 41 percent of the "low achievers," described their political views as left or liberal. Forty-eight percent of the former, but only 38 percent of the latter, indicated general approval of "the emergence of radical student activism in recent years." The use of busing to achieve school integration was endorsed by more than half of the "high achievers," in comparison to just two-fifths of the "low."

Because it has been frequently alleged that federal consulting and research grants tend to make the recipients more conservative, we examined the politics of consultants-grantees—faculty who in the

[45] Institutions were ranked on the basis of a three-item index of academic standing, including SAT scores required for admission (selectivity), research expenditures adjusted for the number of students (research), and total institutional expenditures, also adjusted to a per student basis (affluence). All colleges and universities were arrayed on this index, with raw scores ranging from 3 (highest standing) to 27 (lowest). *Elite schools* here are those with index scores of 3 to 9; the *lowest tier* institutions scored in the 18 to 27 range.

[46] We have described the construction of the liberalism-conservatism scale in a number of other publications. See, for example, "The Politics of Academic Natural Scientists and Engineers," pp. 1092-1099.

twelve months preceding the survey had both served as paid consultants to some agency of the national government and held federal research grants. Some may have become more conservative as a result of these contacts, but professors who consulted for the government and drew on its largesse were still more liberal-left in general political orientation—for example, more critical of government policies in Vietnam and more supportive of the student protests of the late sixties—than were the rank and file of faculty.

The data in Table 4 demonstrate that these differences in political views, between faculty of high and intermediate-to-low academic standing and attainments, extend throughout the several age strata. Opposition to the prevailing U.S. position in Vietnam in 1969, for example, was expressed by 60 percent of professors of intermediate-to-low attainment in the under thirty-five age group, as contrasted to 81 percent of their age mates of high attainment. Forty-seven percent of the former, but 60 percent of the latter, indicated support for the busing of public school children to promote racial integration. In each age group, the "high achievers" are consistently more liberal than the "low." [47]

There seems to be little doubt that the model suggested by the literature on the socially critical posture of achieving intellectuals provides a far more satisfactory guide to understanding political differences between the "top" and the "bottom" levels of the professoriate than does one stemming from application of the class theory of politics. A large number of surveys of professors, from James Leuba's analysis of the factors associated with religious belief through the Carnegie data gathered in 1969, all agree that achievement in higher education, however measured, has been associated with more liberal-to-left views on a wide array of social and political issues. Perhaps most startling of all is the conclusion first presented by Lazarsfeld and Thielens in *The Academic Mind* with respect to support for the rights of Communists and other minorities, and reiterated in our analysis of the Carnegie data with reference, for example, to opposition to the Vietnam War. This conclusion is that faculty consultants for the federal government have been more likely

---

[47] In Table 4, we have applied "breaks" with regard to achievement somewhat different from those used in Table 3. To simplify matters in view of further controls for age, only two attainment categories were used: faculty at elite colleges and universities, and those at the top of the second tier, with five or more professional publications in the two years preceding the Carnegie survey; and all those with fewer than five publications at institutions of academic standing below the elite and upper second tier levels.

Table 4

POLITICAL ORIENTATIONS OF ACADEMICS, BY SCHOLARLY ACHIEVEMENT AND AGE; 1969 CARNEGIE FACULTY SURVEY

(all data presented as percentages of *n*)

	Support Busing for Integration	Support Immediate U.S. Withdrawal from Vietnam or Coalition Government With Viet Cong	1964 Vote for Johnson	1968 Vote		Support "Radical Student Activism"	Very Liberal and Liberal (Liberalism-Conservatism Scale)
				For Humphrey	For left third party		
All faculty							
Achievement dichotomized as:							
High (n=6,552)	54	74	88	69	3	48	52
Intermediate-to-low (n=25,593)	42	54	75	55	2	40	34
Under 35							
High (n=1,602)	60	81	87	72	6	54	63
Intermediate-to-low (n=8,439)	47	60	74	56	4	50	44
35–49							
High (n=3,510)	53	74	89	70	2	50	52
Intermediate-to-low (n=10,953)	40	53	75	56	1	37	33
50 and over							
High (n=1,425)	48	66	87	64	2	36	42
Intermediate-to-low (n=6,075)	40	47	74	50	1	32	24

to align themselves against the government's position on crucial issues than colleagues not on the consulting payroll of the "political establishment."

The "top" of the academic community is more liberal than the "bottom," not because its members are more advantaged in salary, research opportunities, and various perquisites of academic life, of course, but seemingly because as a group their role and orientations are closer to those of the ideal-type intellectual. The fact of greater liberalism among faculty of high attainment and recognition holds because of the essential inapplicability of the class theory in explaining dominant characteristics of professorial politics.

The Divided Professoriate

The disproportionate liberalism of American academics, compared to other occupational groups, and the notably critical orientations of achieving faculty, are well established. The above commentary, however, leaves untouched several key components of professorial politics in the United States which we considered as we structured our 1972 investigation, and these are essential to any general overview of the subject. On the one hand, it must be noted that what we have described is a relatively striking commitment by faculty, especially in view of their middle-class standing, to political positions reflective of egalitarian, change-oriented, and generally liberal perspectives. This is not at all the same as a commitment to political radicalism. "Radical," like most of the other labels so freely applied in political discourse—liberal, conservative, left, right, reactionary, et cetera—admits to a number of different meanings. Central to these is a call for sweeping changes in the basic structure of political life. No study of American academics has shown anything more than a small minority inclined to radical politics. In 1948, for example, Lazarsfeld and Thielens found that fewer than 8 percent of social scientists—the group whose university discipline shows political attitudes farthest left—voted for the left third party candidacies of Henry Wallace and Norman Thomas; about 92 percent backed one of the two conventional major party candidates, Truman or Dewey. Two decades later, amid the political turbulence and unrest especially notable on college campuses, fewer than 3 percent of all professors in the United States, and only 5 percent of social science faculty, cast their ballots for the minor parties of the left. More than 95 professors out of every 100 who went to the polls in November 1968 voted for one of the two major party candidates (in a relatively high turnout, about 90 percent of all those eligible to vote). Just as universities have been seen correctly by many outside observers as centers of relatively liberal and critical politics, so they are criticized frequently by radicals within, again correctly, for being generally unsupportive of revolutionary political changes.

A second important qualifying point bearing on what we have described as the general liberalism of faculty is the existence of sharply patterned political differences within the professoriate. In other words, the faculty as an aggregate group looks liberal when compared to most other occupational strata, but there are large segments in the academic community whose political orientations now, and over the past half century, have not stood to the left of the American political center. We have discussed in a number of publications the exceptionally large internal differentiation of the professoriate by discipline, for example.[48] There is a rather neat progression from the most left of center to the most conservative, running from the social sciences to the humanities, law and the fine arts, through the physical and biological sciences, education and medicine, on to business, engineering, nursing and home economics, and finally to agriculture, the most conservative of the discipline groupings. Within universities, political differences relating to discipline are as great or greater than those between the well-to-do and the poor, between Christians and Jews, or than almost any other group variance in political outlook in the larger society.

Close to two-thirds of those in social science indicated in the 1969 Carnegie survey that they approved of "the rise of radical student activism," as compared to two-fifths in the natural sciences, and only one-fifth in agriculture. About 70 percent of academic social scientists identified themselves as left or liberal, in comparison to 43 percent of the natural scientists and 31 percent of the faculty in business schools. In the 1968 presidential election, Richard Nixon's support ranged from 3 percent among professors of social work, 8 percent among anthropologists, and 14 percent in sociology, to 55 percent in business administration, 62 percent in agriculture and a massive 71 percent among professors of civil engineering. It should also be noted that in 1968 the Republican nominee received a markedly higher proportion of the vote among professors in schools

---

[48] See, in particular, "The Divided Professoriate," pp. 54-55; "Politics of Academic Natural Scientists and Engineers," pp. 1092-1096; and "The Politics of American Political Scientists," pp. 138-140.

of business administration, engineering, agriculture, and various other applied professional disciplines than he did in the public at large.[49]

Disciplines, then, are especially influential in differentiating faculty political orientations, and there are related areas of study, notably those associated with business enterprise and technology, which have shown a consistently conservative bent.[50] The discipline variations are especially striking when one recognizes that the respective faculties work in a common institution, receive comparable remuneration, and have similar social and economic status. These variations testify to the extent to which contrasting subject matters are associated with patterns of recruitment and socialization which have an extraordinary political impact.

Differences in political orientation by age group are also especially striking in the professoriate, with older faculty much more conservative than their junior colleagues in all types of university settings, in all groups of disciplines. Together, age and area of study produce massive variations in political orientation. For instance, 72 percent of social scientists under 35 years of age are located in the most liberal categories of the liberalism-conservatism scale, in contrast to 15 percent of business, engineering and agriculture school professors who are over age 50. Eighty percent of the former, but only 34 percent of the latter, opposed United States policies in Vietnam in 1969. The Carnegie survey shows that 62 percent of senior professors in the above-mentioned applied disciplines backed Richard Nixon in 1968, as against only 18 percent of young social scientists.

The academic world is diverse politically. Attention to its overall liberalism can obscure its internal political heterogeneity and the presence of some enduring centers of conservative politics. Almost certainly, one of the reasons why universities were so fragmented politically by the events of the late sixties is that they are so internally diverse. It is hard to imagine any other institution in American society in which those responsible for decision making—as faculty are generally responsible in a wide range of colleges and universities

---

[49] This statement, unmodified, is somewhat misleading since Wallace drew 13.5 percent of the vote in the electorate, but was backed by only 1 percent of professors. Still, it is striking to note that, for example, Nixon's 60 percent support among all faculty in the engineering disciplines exceeded the combined Nixon and Wallace support among the general public.

[50] It should be noted that studies of undergraduates show comparably sharp differences in political attitudes by field of concentration. Students majoring in the business-related professional disciplines are markedly more conservative than those in the social sciences and humanities. For a review of these studies, see Lipset, *Rebellion in the University* (Boston: Little, Brown & Co., 1972), especially pp. 80-123.

—are so sharply at odds over all manner of core political assumptions. This fact of sharp internal differences is as important to a general understanding of the politics of American academics as recognition of their collective disproportionately liberal stance, and the reasons for it.

As we approached our study of faculty politics in 1972, we were aware of a past record of political orientations and behavior that was likely to make for a more complex pattern than some outside observers casually assumed. It would be surprising, we felt, if McGovern did not do better in the professoriate than in the public at large, but a professoriate generally at odds politically could be expected to manifest a substantial internal division in the 1972 balloting.

One final factor made the 1972 presidential politics of academics especially intriguing, the effects or spin-offs of the intense politicization and divisiveness which universities have experienced over the last decade. The issues of student activism and campus politicization had divided many colleges and universities long before the 1972 elections. Throughout the country during the late sixties, faculty meetings, which once could hardly attract a quorum, took place in large assembly halls, often remaining in session for many hours. On a number of campuses from Berkeley to Cambridge, open faculty "parties" or caucuses were formed, seeking to affect university policy by winning majorities at faculty meetings or in elections. In a similar fashion, many national academic associations were divided into caucuses. The left-wing factions sought to make concern for public policy and social change a recognized activity in the group. The more moderate forces in turn organized to oppose what they viewed as unwelcome politicization. Many academics who had been identified in the past as liberals and Democrats found themselves in alliance with conservatives to prevent actions they considered a threat to the integrity of the university and scholarship. In our analysis of data from the 1969 Carnegie survey, we found significant groups of faculty normally associated with a liberal view on political questions drawing back from a "liberal" view of militant faculty-student activism.

Impressionistically, we had noted prior to conducting our 1972 survey a tendency for some faculty who had expressed concern about the effects of campus activism and politicization to identify George McGovern with these trends, in part perhaps because more militant students and younger faculty often formed the core of his visibly active supporters in university communities. By taking a strong anti-war position, and identifying with college-based activism, McGovern was able to mobilize support which helped win Democratic primaries and precinct denomination meetings in nonprimary states. But in so doing, it appears to us, he had alienated the segment of traditionally liberal national Democrats who reacted negatively to the university activism of recent years and to the pressures it injected into university affairs.

Opinion was divided about protests and demonstrations against the war, some of which resulted in the seizure of buildings and similar confrontations, and about all of the attendant arguments concerning the use of police, the proper role and responsibilities of the university, et cetera. Demands for "affirmative action" or for quotas in the hiring of blacks and women to professional positions and in the admitting of students were seen by some as appropriate university actions on behalf of equality and by others as assaults on meritocracy. Charges of racism within the academy and insistence upon vigorous steps to eradicate it were applauded by proponents as essential to full freedom for blacks, and rejected by opponents as inviting "smear tactics" and thus posing a threat to academic freedom. These and related conflicts over the last half decade or so have produced sharp separations among faculty that divide opinion very differently from the conventional liberal-conservative axis.

Such intra-campus controversies seem linked to a broader ideological division in the American intellectual community. It is far less meaningful to ask of an American intellectual today "Are you liberal or conservative?" than to ask "Are you *Commentary* or *New York Review of Books?*" Some of the strains in this division are old, but others are very new, products of the massive changes which have occurred in the American political agenda in recent years. They show a change from intellectual residues of who bears responsibility for the cold war to the intellectual boundaries of "equality," for whom, through what channels, at what expense? On the whole, "*Commentary* intellectuals" rejected McGovern, while those of the *New York Review of Books* embraced him.

For American college professors, then, as for the intellectual community at large, the 1972 presidential election, the issues it contained and the candidates representing these issues, promised to involve something more than a simple liberal-conservative split. In particular, we expected among academics an interesting tension between disproportionately liberal inclinations of long standing and the "frontlash-backlash" generated by activism and the "new campus politics" of the last half decade.

Before turning directly to our survey of faculty political orientations in 1972, we should examine the 1972 election itself, and the larger dynamic of American electoral politics. While the general ideological orientations of professors, and their responses to new issues felt keenly in the campus context, are important, so too is the national political context. Forces operating upon the body politic generally could not help but influence the professoriate. They also define a broader context in which faculty electoral responses can be more effectively assessed.

2

THE FABRIC OF CONTEMPORARY AMERICAN ELECTORAL POLITICS

Like their fellow Americans, college faculty cast presidential ballots in November 1972 as the United States was passing through an extraordinary transition period in its electoral history. Few observers could fail to detect that the old electoral order had been turned on its ear. Here was a Democratic presidential nominee ending a campaign in which he had virtually written off the states of the old Confederacy. Here was a Republican candidate concluding his quest for reelection with the tacit backing of a large segment of organized labor. The Republican party, so long and so surely considered home to the American "establishment," had proclaimed itself the champion of forgotten "middle Americans" and had apparently gained politically from charges of elitism within the Democratic party's leadership. But in the long list of indicators of electoral change, one item stood out as the most revealing. For the second time in eight years, a presidential candidate who might have expected to win, at best, a modest majority had become the recipient of a massive victory, the winner by one of the largest margins in American presidential history. More impressive than the issues of 1972 or than long-term group realignments is the appearance of landslides which, according to the conventional "rules" of our presidential politics, should not have happened. The atmosphere of "unnatural landslides" permeated all facets of American politics in 1972, including that of the university campuses.

American two-party politics has in the past assumed, with fair correspondence to reality, the following sequence: Both the Democratic and the Republican parties, confident in the support of their respective "faithfuls," have looked for presidential nominees who would be able to build from the secure base to a majority. The search for supporters beyond those who could be counted upon has typically produced appeals to sectional, ethnic and class groupings supposedly susceptible to courtship. Insofar as the search has been based on issues, it has involved an effort to capture the ground where most of the people are.

In other words, our working model has assumed two national parties engaged in accommodationist politics. Clinton Rossiter put it this way, that

> they [the two major parties] are creatures of compromise, coalitions of interest in which principle is muted and often even silenced. They are vast, gaudy, friendly umbrellas under which all Americans, whoever and wherever and however-minded they may be, are invited to stand for the sake of being counted in the next election. The parties, moderate and tolerant and self-contradictory to a fault, are interested in the votes of men, not in their principles. . . . The task that they have uppermost in mind is the construction of a victorious majority, and in a country as large and diverse as ours this calls for programs and candidates having as nearly universal an appeal as the imperatives of politics will permit. It calls, that is to say, for a gallant attempt by each party to mirror the entire American electorate. . . .[1]

The model which emerged from observation of the American parties nationally, then, casts them as coalition-minded, seeking a majority from the extraordinary heterogeneity of the country on the basis of loose appeals and not sharply defined, ideologically structured programs. The parties have been seen operating from an assumption of multi-structured mobilization. A majority could not be secured by drawing lines neatly around any single axis, so it was sought by attempting to mobilize varying segments of the electorate through diverse appeals across a series of axes of conflict.

This point is sometimes made by stating that the national parties have competed for "the center." But the concept of a center in issue or ideological terms is somewhat confusing because it suggests a single continuum upon which voters are arrayed. In post-New Deal nomenclature, this would mean that Republicans as the more conservative party and Democrats as the more liberal have sought in their presidential appeals to attract voters whose issue concerns are

---

[1] Clinton Rossiter, *Parties and Politics in America* (Ithaca, N. Y.: Cornell University Press, 1960), p. 11.

neither decisively liberal or conservative, but rather are near the center of the continuum. The notion of a search for the center would be fine if the mix of issues, in fact, would generally fit any such single continuum. We know, however, that reality does not submit to such analytic neatness. For example, in the principal Republican issue appeals in 1952 of "communism, corruption, and Korea," where was the center? What is the liberal or conservative position on corruption? What was it on the Korean War?

The issue mix, typically, does not lend itself to "more than" or "less than" along a single ideological or quasi-ideological dimension. Donald Stokes caught a facet of this when he noted that

> the empirical point that needs to be made is that many of the issues that agitate our politics do not involve even a shriveled set of two alternatives of governmental action. The corruption issue of 1952 did not find the Democrats taking one position and the Republicans another. And neither were some voters in favor of corruption while others were against it. If we are to speak of a dimension at all, both parties and all voters were located at a single point— the position of virtue in government. . . . To emphasize the difference involved here let us call *"position issues"* those that involve advocacy of government actions from a set of alternatives over which a distribution of voter preferences is defined. And borrowing a term from Kurt Lewin let us call *"valence issues"* those that merely involve the linking of the parties with some condition that is positively or negatively valued by the electorate. . . . It will not do simply to exclude valence issues from the discussion of party competition. The people's choice too often depends upon them. At least in American presidential elections of the past generation it is remarkable how many valence issues have held the center of the stage.[2]

It may be possible in a general way to locate the center with respect to a cluster of related issues, but there may be other clusters each with quite different centers. Furthermore, the notion of a center makes no sense at all with reference to valence issues. For these reasons, it is more precise to describe the traditional mechanics of American two-party politics as comprising a series of issue appeals designed to be majoritarian.

---

[2] Donald E. Stokes, "Spacial Models of Party Competition," as reprinted in Angus Campbell et al., *Elections and the Political Order* (New York: John Wiley & Sons, 1966), pp. 170-171.

So much of the historical literature on the American parties has noted their efforts to put together a majority by being "all things to all people." Thus, the parties are described as "tweedledum and tweedledee," imagery which connotes superficial dissimilarity masking essential similarity. There is not, we have been told repeatedly by critics, "a dime's worth of difference" between the Republicans and Democrats. Exaggerated as such statements are, they stand as efforts to capture the characteristics of a party system operating normally according to the dictates of accommodation.

If both parties competing for the presidency conform to the model described above, under what circumstances can—and indeed have—landslides occurred? [3] Two principal circumstances, alone or in concert, have been decisive. In one instance, salient events may be decisively stacked against one party. For example, in 1932 neither the Republicans nor the Democrats favored economic collapse and depression, but the Republicans were in office when the collapse occurred and were necessarily associated with it. A second, different source of landslides occurs when one party is blessed with a candidate of unusual personal standing and popularity—or more generally, when there is a decisive gap between the personal appeal of the contenders. Thus, Eisenhower's victory of 1956 appears more than anything else as a personal tribute, a product of his exceptional individual popularity. And back in 1904 Alton B. Parker was no match for dynamic "Teddy" Roosevelt. It should be added that the majority party can secure a major victory with a more modest advantage in candidate appeal or in the weight of political events than can the minority party. The party with the larger share of identifiers begins with a built-in advantage. In any event, the elections of 1904, 1932 and 1956 may be taken as examples of "natural" landslides. They are perfectly compatible with the accommodationist politics model.

The elections of 1972 and 1964 do not, however, present these conditions. Neither Nixon nor Johnson benefited from high personal affection across the electorate, or projected charismatic appeal. Sensing that voters did not much like either candidate, for example, a reporter for the *New York Times* had the Daniel Yankelovich survey organization include in its 1972 questionnaire an item which gave respondents the opportunity to indicate disinterest in both contenders. The question was: "Now, forgetting about politics, whom do you find more attractive as a personality, Nixon, McGovern, or

---

[3] For convenience, we may think of a landslide election as one in which the winning candidate enjoys at least a 10 percentage point margin over his principal rival.

neither one?" As is shown below, an exceptionally high proportion of respondents—about a third—"voted" for "neither." [4]

	Nixon	McGovern	Neither	Not Sure
Survey of October 1-12, 1972	34	26	32	8
Survey of October 15-24, 1972	33	23	37	7

Moreover, in both years the general social and economic climate did not decisively favor either party. In 1972, with the country at war and the economy unsettled, with a climate of considerable pessimism concerning the adequacy of American institutions and processes, and with the emerging Watergate scandal, one could hardly argue that the Republicans were linked to an overall national circumstance so positively valued by the electorate as to make them, as the incumbent party, virtually impregnable.

Here, then, is the basis for the feeling, variously expressed, that the 1972 Nixon landslide, like that of his predecessor eight years earlier, was "unlikely." The landslides should not have occurred if the behavior of both parties had conformed to the accommodationist model. But occur they did. These two presidential elections are among the most one-sided in American electoral history, as Table 5 demonstrates.

Ordered by the percentage point spread between the winner and the runner-up, the 1972 and 1964 elections ranked fourth and fifth respectively in a list of ten record landslides. Measured simply in terms of the victor's percentage of the total vote cast, the Johnson and Nixon victories were the two largest in American history.[5] Two of the most imposing presidential victories were achieved, then, by nominees not known for their personal popularity with the electorate and not the beneficiaries of especially fortunate blends of social cir-

---

[4] Surveys conducted by Daniel Yankelovich, sponsored by the *New York Times* and *Time*, cited by Peter B. Natchez, "The Unlikely Landslide: Issues and Voters in the 1972 Election" (A paper presented at the annual meeting of the New England Political Science Association, Boston, Massachusetts, April 27, 1973), p. 3. The numbers responding to the question were 2,323 in the first survey, 3,010 in the second. For a discussion of this phenomenon, see Lipset and Earl Raab, "The Election and the National Mood," *Commentary*, vol. 55 (January 1973), pp. 43-44.

[5] While the subject cannot be examined here, it should be noted that nine of the ten record landslides in American political history have occurred in the twentieth century. On the whole, presidential contests were much closer in the nineteenth century, especially between 1876 and 1900.

Table 5

U.S. PRESIDENTIAL ELECTIONS IN WHICH THE WINNER'S MARGIN WAS HIGHEST

(rank ordered)

Year	Principal Candidates	Winner's Share of the Total Vote Cast	Winner's Margin Over Principal Challenger
1920	Harding-Cox	60.3%	26.2%
1924	Coolidge-Davis	54.0	25.2
1936	Roosevelt-Landon	60.8	24.3
1972	Nixon-McGovern	60.8	23.2
1964	Johnson-Goldwater	61.1	22.6
1904	Roosevelt-Parker	56.4	18.8
1932	Roosevelt-Hoover	57.4	17.8
1928	Hoover-Smith	58.2	17.4
1832	Jackson-Clay	54.5	17.0
1956	Eisenhower-Stevenson	57.4	15.4

cumstance. Nixon's 1972 landslide is all the more striking because it was achieved by a nominee of the minority party. The only other one-sided triumph listed in Table 5 for a minority party nominee was Eisenhower's 1956 victory. But Eisenhower had built his political career upon being "above [partisan] politics," whereas Nixon was the quintessential Republican partisan leader.

That the landslides of 1972 and 1964 did in fact take place requires one of two explanations: either they were deviant cases, products of a peculiar mix of personalities and events not likely to recur, and hence are of interest solely as aberrations, as "political museum pieces," or they followed from some fundamental, structural changes bearing upon party role in national electoral politics, which point to a significant weakening if not a collapse of assumptions and practices associated with accommodationist politics. Either the old rules hold and the landslides were merely flukes, or new rules are being written. If it is the latter, then perhaps observers a decade hence, in their retrospective analysis of these two landslides, will consider them far from unnatural. Unlikely under the old rules, they may conform easily to the dictates of a new structure of national inter-party competition. It is the latter possibility which commands our attention. For if a basic rewriting is indeed occurring, it carries importance far beyond the results of these two contests.

Sources of a Changing Dynamic

During and after the one-sided presidential contests of 1964 and 1972, we have had a plethora of commentary expressing concern as to how and why each occurred. When the candidate of one of the major parties loses by sixteen million votes (as did Goldwater in 1964), or by seventeen and one half million (McGovern in 1972), it is hard to avoid the conclusion that something went wrong. And it is not at all hard to locate a variety of specific circumstances, events, and errors which are associated with the devastatingly lopsided results. Some of the problems experienced by the losers are obviously chance occurrences. Few would argue, for example, that any structural attributes of American politics accounted for McGovern's selection of a vice presidential running mate who would subsequently be embarrassed by revelations of previous mental illness. But the possibility must be seriously entertained that many of the specific events associated with the record defeats were but surface reflections of some underlying change in the dynamic of American national politics. When twice in eight years, first a Republican and then a Democratic presidential nominee loses by near-record proportions to an opponent not known for high personal popularity and not blessed by especially favorable political circumstances, and when the losing candidates manifest strikingly similar patterns, a serious search for some fundamental, long-term causation is indicated. This is especially so since the consequences of such unnatural landslides for American political life are so profound. In effect, large numbers of voters in 1964 and 1972 concluded that they did not really have a choice—that there was only one acceptable, if not especially appealing, possibility.

As we have examined the possibility that the recent unlikely landslides reflect a changed dynamic, two broad sets of developments have been identified as potentially the most significant. One starts from the recognition that the "citizenry parties"[6] as bundles of electoral loyalties are coming apart, unraveling, disaggregating. The other focuses upon the political role of the college-educated new middle class generally, the growth of one stratum of party activists

---

[6] We use *citizenry parties* interchangeably with *the parties in the electorate*. As has often been noted, political party is variously used to describe formal organizational structure, to describe groups of elected officials who accept the party label, or to designate those who think of themselves as adherents of the party and/or give regular support to the party's nominees. Citizenry party contains this latter group.

and an ideological polarization of ascendant Republican and Democratic activist groups.

Disaggregation, Not Realignment

For some time now, politicians, journalists and scholars alike have been attracted to the idea that the United States may be again on the brink of a "critical realignment," a massive restructuring of electoral loyalties in which the relative standing of the contending parties is significantly altered for the long term. During the 1950s, discussion centered pretty much upon the prospects for an "emerging Republican majority." In one ecstatic moment in 1952, Senator Robert A. Taft decreed that "the Democratic party will never win another national election until it solves the problem of the suburbs." As competent an observer as Professor Edward Banfield assumed a 60 percent Republican suburban plurality and hence predicted that the Democrats' electoral advantage in metropolitan areas would disappear shortly after 1956 and that the imbalance between city and suburban populations would be so great by 1975 that the Republican metropolitan plurality would exceed two million.[7] If being a Democrat and having high socioeconomic status were in some way contradictory, then the move to suburbia which symbolizes a rise in socioeconomic status should precipitate a conversion to Republicanism. Suburbanites as people of high socioeconomic status were naturally more conservative, and the Grand Old Party (GOP) was the more conservative of the two parties.[8] In 1964, however, the partisan balance was supposedly tipped more decisively in the Democrats' favor.

Following Goldwater's massive defeat, the view was frequently expressed that the Grand Old Party might not survive as a viable contender, that a period of more complete Democratic ascendancy had probably been inaugurated. James Reston wrote in the *New York Times* of November 4, 1964 that "he [Senator Goldwater] had wrecked his party for a long time to come. . . ." And Angus Campbell, a keen student of electoral politics, examined the Survey Research Center's 1964 election study data and concluded that the United

---

[7] Edward Banfield, "The Changing Political Environment of City Planning" (A paper delivered at the American Political Science Association meeting, 1956).

[8] Louis Harris, *Is There a Republican Majority?* (New York: Harper and Brothers, 1954) presents one of the more complete statements of "conversion." See also Harry Gersh, "The New Suburbanites of the Fifties," *Commentary*, vol. 17 (March 1954), p. 217; and Frederick Lewis Allen, "The Big Change in Suburbia," pt. 2, *Harpers*, July 1954, p. 50.

States was quite possibly entering "a period of party realignment which will increase the prevailing Democratic advantage in the party balance." [9]

Just a half decade later, however, the lines of commentary again shifted with talk of significant partisan realignment occurring on the Republicans' behalf. Kevin Phillips's much discussed book, *The Emerging Republican Majority,* is the most elaborate exposition of this theory. But such obviously partisan explanations would have been of little moment had they not found general confirmation in the reports of more detached journalists and social scientists. Andrew Hacker, for one, predicted that "the [Republican] party may well begin to chalk up majorities as it has not since the days of Calvin Coolidge." [10]

Interestingly enough, following Richard Nixon's enormous electoral victory in 1972 there has been little discussion of any such critical realignment. The prime reason for this seems to be that it has at last become obvious that large numbers of voters are not so much changing their "residence" from one party to another for a protracted duration as they are becoming partisan "transients." To be sure, realignments are occurring, but a major critical realignment, establishing a new majority coalition, no longer appears in the offing. Evidence that the major shift occurring in national politics involves partisan disaggregation rather than partisan realignment has become overwhelming.

The psychological cement which has bound voters to parties is crumbling. It has not collapsed completely, and will not do so. But it has weakened so significantly as to raise seriously the question of whether the United States will experience in the foreseeable future a critical realignment of the order of those which occurred in the 1890s or in the 1930s.

Evidence of a weakening of party ties is abundant. For one thing, a growing proportion of the electorate—when asked the now familiar "Generally speaking in politics as of today, do you consider yourself. . . ?"—has come to answer "independent" rather than "Democrat" or "Republican." Both Gallup and the Survey Research Center of Michigan found that self-described independents began outnumbering Republican identifiers in the latter half of the sixties, for the first time since the inauguration of systematic voter surveys.

[9] Angus Campbell, "Interpreting the Presidential Victory," in Milton C. Cummings, Jr., ed., *The National Election of 1964* (Washington, D. C.: The Brookings Institution, 1966), pp. 278-279.

[10] Andrew Hacker, "Is There a New Republican Majority?" *Commentary,* vol. 48 (November 1969), p. 70.

By 1972, about one-third of the population was consistently found adopting the independent label, with about one quarter describing themselves as Republicans and four in ten as Democrats. Throughout the 1940s and 1950s independents had hovered around 20 percent of the electorate.

College-educated voters have consistently comprised a higher proportion of self-described independents than the public at large, but the growth of independent status in the former group has increased dramatically in recent years. In 1944, according to Gallup surveys, 47 percent of college-trained voters identified as Republicans, 31 percent as Democrats, and 21 percent as independents. As recently as 1960, there had been relatively little change in the college-educated population. The proportion of Republicans was down slightly, that of Democrats up marginally, while independents had become about one-fourth of the total. Over the last half decade, however, independents have become "the largest party" among college-educated Americans. According to 1972 Gallup data, 37 percent of voters who had attended college described themselves as independents, 32 percent as Republicans and 31 percent as Democrats.[11]

Not only are larger numbers of voters describing themselves as independents, but there is also an actual increase in independent electoral behavior—specifically, in split-ticket voting, where an elector casts his ballot for Republican candidate(s) in one set of offices and at the same time supports Democratic nominee(s) for others. This is the crucial variable. We agree with DeVries and Tarrance that "the real test of the voter's independence is whether or not he splits his

---

[11] In this and the above references to party identification as revealed by Gallup data, we have utilized a number of surveys in each of the calendar years referred to. To increase the number of cases upon which the percentages are based and to reduce the effect of random variations from one single study to another, five separate surveys, in the same year and each asking the party identification question in exactly the same language, have been combined and treated for purposes of this analysis as a single study. This technique is followed by the Gallup organization, and was used effectively by V. O. Key in *The Responsible Electorate* (Cambridge, Mass.: Harvard University Press, 1966). For further application, see Ladd, Charles D. Hadley, and Lauriston R. King, "The American Party Coalitions: Social Change and Partisan Alignments, 1935-1970" (A paper presented at the 66th Annual Meeting of the American Political Science Association, Los Angeles, California, September 8-12, 1970); and by the same authors, "A New Political Realignment?" *The Public Interest*, Spring 1971, pp. 46-63. The Gallup organization has commented on this procedure in *Gallup Opinion Index*, Report No. 36 (June 1968): "The findings for political affiliation . . . are based on over 10,000 cases, with several surveys being combined. Results based on 1,500 cases (the minimum number of cases in a typical Gallup survey) are highly reliable, but this large sample of 10,000 cases enables us to give detailed breakdowns. For example, we can have reliable information not only by age groups, but age groups by region of the country."

ticket. A voter may say he is an independent, but this can be confirmed only by his actual voting behavior."[12]

Walter Dean Burnham has plotted the number of congressional districts producing split-party outcomes (the vote for President going one way and the vote for congressman the other) throughout the twentieth century. His data show a marked secular increase in this manifestation of split-ticket voting in the contemporary period. Thus, voters gave a majority to one party in the presidential balloting and to another in House of Representatives' contests in fewer than 20 percent of the congressional districts in 1952. This pattern of split-party results was observed in 32 percent of the congressional districts in 1968 and reached a new record of 42 percent in 1972.[13] Burnham maintains that although data have not been compiled for the period prior to 1900, "it seems safe to assume that between the Civil War and the turn of the century, split results existed normally in less than 5 percent of the congressional districts, and never—or almost never—exceeded 10 percent of such districts." There has been a long-term increase in split presidential-congressional outcomes, but an especially dramatic jump during the last decade.

Howard Reiter has provided data on the incidence of split outcomes involving two other offices, governorships and U.S. Senate seats. In the 1920s, he found, there was a divergent outcome (Republicans victors in the Senate vote, Democrats in the gubernatorial balloting, or vice versa) on average in about 20 percent of the states holding these two elections simultaneously. The proportion of split outcomes in the 1940s was essentially the same. It increased moderately in the 1950s but dramatically over the past decade. Thus, 44 percent of states with simultaneous gubernatorial and senatorial elections in 1960 produced split outcomes, 56 percent in 1964, 59 percent in 1966, 60 percent in 1968, 46 percent in 1970, and 50 percent in 1972.[14]

These data provide only a very crude indication of increases in the level of split-ticket voting. An election in which 49 percent of

---

[12] Walter DeVries and V. Lance Tarrance, *The Ticket-Splitter: A New Force in American Politics* (Grand Rapids, Mich.: William B. Eerdmans, 1972), p. 23. This volume provides a useful collection of data on the actual increase in the incidents of split-ticket voting.

[13] Walter Dean Burnham, *Critical Elections and the Mainsprings of American Politics* (New York: W. W. Norton & Co., 1970), p. 109. The 1972 data were made available to the authors by Professor Burnham.

[14] The data through 1968 are from Howard Reiter, an unpublished paper presented at the John Fitzgerald Kennedy School of Government, Harvard University, 1969 and have been reprinted in DeVries and Tarrance, *The Ticket-Splitter*, p. 31.

voters in a district give their support to a Republican presidential nominee and a Democratic congressional candidate, and one where 70 percent of the electorate endorse a Republican for President while 70 percent vote Democratic in the House contest, are classified as the same. Both, that is, are described as involving split-party outcomes, even though the apparent incidence of ticket splitting was minimal in the first case and very large in the second. These indicators, nevertheless, provide a general demonstration of the pronounced decrease in straight-party voting.

Survey data provide other measures of the incidence of independent voting—defined both in terms of a split ticket in a given election, and of moving back and forth between the parties over time for a single office such as President. In each of their presidential election year surveys since 1952, researchers at the University of Michigan's Survey Research Center have asked respondents whether they "have . . . always voted for the same party or have . . . voted for different parties for President." In 1952, 71 percent of respondents in the national sample indicated that they had always or "mostly" voted for the same party. Sixteen years later, the SRC reported that the proportion of consistent Democratic and Republican presidential voters had dropped to just 56 percent of the electorate.

The best indicator, perhaps, of the level of independent voting is the frequency with which individual electors support Democrats for some offices while backing Republicans for others. We have no fully reliable data prior to the 1940s, but DeVries and Tarrance have estimated that proportions of only 20 percent or so of the electorate in the split-ticket category were common.[15] In 1948, Gallup for the first time asked a national sample a question permitting systematic assessment of the incidence of straight-ticket voting: "Did you vote a straight ticket—that is, did you vote for all candidates of the one party—or did you vote a split ticket, that is, did you vote for some candidates of one party and some of the other?" Sixty-two percent of respondents described themselves as straight-ticket voters, 38 percent as ticket-splitters.[16] Gallup repeated the same question in subsequent surveys in the 1950s and early 1960s, and found little change in the proportions. Thus, in 1964, a post-election survey showed 59 percent having voted a straight ticket, 41 percent having split their ballot. Since 1964, however, the percentage of ticket-

---

[15] DeVries and Tarrance, *The Ticket-Splitter*, p. 22.

[16] American Institute of Public Opinion (AIPO) Survey No. 432, November 1, 1948. The data were made available through the Roper Center for Public Opinion Research, Williamstown, Massachusetts.

splitters has increased dramatically: According to Gallup, it reached 56 percent of the electorate in 1968 and 62 percent in 1972.[17] Over the last decade, then, the proportion of the electorate splitting their ballots in presidential election years has jumped from roughly two-fifths to nearly two-thirds.

Michigan's Survey Research Center has asked a question similar to Gallup's, but limited to state and local races. Since presidential elections, with their focus on candidate personalities and programs, are known to manifest the highest incidence of nonparty-oriented voting, we would expect the SRC question to yield higher proportions of straight-ticket voters than the Gallup question which covered the total spectrum of elections. But the underlying pattern of a substantial drop in straight-party voting in recent years remains the same. Thus, the 1952 SRC survey reported 73 percent of the electorate as "party regulars" at the state and local level. In 1956, the proportion was 71 percent, and in 1960, 73 percent. But in 1968, it dropped 20 points, to just 53 percent of the electorate.

By all measures, party ties have grown markedly weaker. This appears to be a long-term decline, with a dramatic drop-off in the last half decade. A larger segment of the electorate is describing itself as independent, and more importantly is behaving independently, in the sense of regularly dividing its support between the parties. Why, then, is this change occurring? What are its precipitants?

One set of answers involves the changing character of the electorate, and related to this, changes in the structure of political communications. The last two decades have seen an extraordinary increase in the proportion of the population which has had formal higher education. The number currently enrolled in colleges and universities increased from just over two million in 1950 to more than eight million in 1971;[18] and the proportion of the population twenty-five years and older who had attended college increased from 12 percent in 1947 to 23 percent in 1972.[19] Just over a quarter of the voting age population in 1972 had attended institutions of higher education. In one sense, the simple percentage figures may under-

[17] The 1964 data are from AIPO Survey No. 701, November 4, 1964; for 1968, AIPO Survey No. 771, November 7, 1968; and for 1972, AIPO Survey No. 860, November 8, 1972.

[18] U.S. Bureau of the Census, *Statistical Abstract of the United States: 1972* (Washington, D. C.: Government Printing Office, 1972), p. 108.

[19] U.S. Bureau of the Census, "Educational Attainment: March 1972," *Current Population Reports*, series T-20, no. 243 (Washington, D. C.: Government Printing Office, 1972), p. 1.

state the magnitude of the change which has occurred in the proportion of the electorate with formal higher education. In 1972, about thirty-five million Americans had attended colleges and universities, and they constitute a group that is more politically active than the rest of the population—voting more regularly, participating more frequently in primary and other intra-party candidate selection activities.

One effect of this "higher education explosion" has been to extend dramatically the proportion of the population which feels no need for parties as active intermediaries in the voting decision. Higher levels of information bearing on political issues and hence a higher measure of "issue orientation," along with a general feeling of confidence in one's ability to judge candidates and their programs apart from party links, are promoted by the experience of higher education. The college-educated voter, in comparison with the population at large, tends to be issue oriented, and the issue-oriented voter is an independent voter. We have already noted that a much higher proportion of college-educated Americans than of the public generally describe themselves as independents. Even more striking, however, is the greater incidence of the split-ticket voting among those who have had higher education. In 1968, according to Gallup, only 34 percent of the college educated voted a straight ticket compared with 48 percent of the high-school and grade-school educated. The extraordinary increases in formal higher education have contributed to a growing reservoir of people inclined to independent voting.

Important as the above consideration is, there is a danger in discussing it out of context. The decline of "party regularity" is not a response exclusively to some mysterious event which occurs when one walks through the doors of a college classroom. The data on higher education are simply a convenient vehicle for indicating that there has been a substantial increase in the proportion of the population with formal training in the world of issues and ideas. There are certainly other ways in which this training can be gained.

In a sense related to the increase in formal education as a precipitant of independent electoral behavior is the development of the electronic communications media as the principal source of political information.[20] The prominence of the electronic media serves to promote partisan "irregularity" in two ways. Party activists are dis-

---

[20] The Survey Research Center has asked respondents in its election year surveys, "Of all these ways of following the campaign, which would you say you got the most information from—newspaper, radio, T.V., or magazines?" In 1952, just 32 percent indicated that television was the prime source. By 1968, however, the proportion was nearly two-thirds (64 percent).

placed as the primary source of political information relevant to candidate assessment for the rank and file of the population. With attention focused so much on the style and personal attributes of the contenders, the role of party ties is necessarily weakened. In an age of television, candidates are brought into voters' living rooms. As personal images become more salient, the importance of the party label to the voting decision must lessen. An electorate, in short, characterized by a high level of formal education, and which secures a highly personalized view of contenders with television as intermediary, will be bound less by partisan identification in its electoral behavior. There seems no prospect in this connection of a reversal of the erosion of party cement. Rather, the process is more likely to accelerate.

A second, quite different source of partisan disaggregation stems from the breakup of a series of group alignments with the parties, some extending back to the New Deal, other to the early years of American political experience. This subject is so large as to go well beyond the boundaries of the present study, but at the same time so central to the dynamic of contemporary American politics that it requires brief discussion here.

The attachments and interests of ethnic groups have always been a prime factor in defining the composition of the American citizenry parties. Today, powerful forces are at work obliterating one ethnic cleavage and putting another in its place. Put crudely, but not inaccurately, in American national life it is now black versus white, no longer Protestant (old stock, western Europe) versus Catholic (new stock, eastern and southern Europe). The Democrats for so long gave something concrete to the ethnocultural groups we describe by one of their characteristics, Catholicism. For example, they made Alfred E. Smith, an Irish Catholic, their presidential nominee in 1928, extending recognition, acceptance, and legitimacy. In return, they received regular electoral support. With the New Deal, Catholic group attachments to the Democratic party were reinforced by economic attachments, because most Catholics were in the economic classes which benefited to the greatest extent from the new social policies. The attachment of Catholics to the Democrats, of course, goes back far beyond the years of Smith and Roosevelt. In terms of services rendered and electoral support received, it is correct to describe the Democrats as the Catholic party (representing a decisive majority of Catholic Americans) since the 1840s.

By the 1960s, however, the position of Catholics in American life had changed. Many had moved up the socioeconomic ladder, were now "haves" rather than "have nots." They were less and less a beneficiary group, more a contributing group, in Democratic welfare policies. Perhaps even more important, most Catholics were no longer "have nots" in status terms, having gained a large measure of acceptance into national life. Throughout much of American history, Protestant versus Catholic was an adequate shorthand summary for the principal ethnic division in the United States. It is no longer. The only politically important ethnic chasm in American national politics today is racial. The Democratic party, as a result of these developments, can no longer count upon status and economic services as a cement to secure Catholics to its coalition. In 1972, for the first time since at least the 1930s when survey data became available, a majority of Catholic Americans voted for the Republican presidential nominee.

Ethnic group attachments to the parties are not the only attachments to crumble. Region-linked loyalties, most notably that of the South to the Democratic party, are in a state of disarray. The century-old regional fidelity of the South to the Democratic party had three great supports. The one best understood is the mixture of experiences surrounding race and the Civil War. The Democratic party came to function as the instrument of white supremacy and regional loyalty. But important as this prop was, it could not have sustained one-partyism for so long by itself. Parallel support was provided by the section's status as a predominantly rural and farming area in those years when the dominant national development centered around industrial nation building. Because the Republicans were quickly established after the Civil War as the principal partisan instrument of the interests surrounding industrialization, the Democratic party was the obvious vehicle for the dissenting interests of the agricultural South. The old Confederacy was the last major section to industrialize. The strength of these two supports naturally permitted construction of a third, that of tradition. Quite tangible interests underlay the South's commitment to the Democratic party, but once established that commitment had a life of its own. For a southerner growing up in, say, 1920, Democratic allegiance was "natural." Was not everyone around Democratic?

Today the first two props have been kicked out, and the third, while still in place, is experiencing immense strains and is being warped in strange ways. Since the 1940s and especially since 1961, the Democratic party nationally has been giving stronger support to the attack on racial inequities than the Republicans. Thus race, which led the region to the Democratic party, is now leading it away.

Table 6

SOUTHERN PRESIDENTIAL VOTE, BY PARTY, COMPARING REGIONAL TO NATIONAL DEMOCRATIC VOTE, 1944-1972

	South [a]			Democratic Percentage of the Vote Nationally	Percentage Difference Between the Democratic Regional (Southern) and National Vote [b]
	Demo-cratic	Repub-lican	Other		
1944	69	31	1	46	+ 23
1948	52	29	18 [c]	50	+ 2
1952	51	49	—	44	+ 7
1956	48	51	1	42	+ 6
1960	48	49	4 [d]	50	− 2
1964	52	48	—	61	− 9
1968	31	36	32 [e]	43	− 12
1972	30	70	—	38	− 8

[a] South here includes the eleven states of the old Confederacy plus Kentucky and Oklahoma.

[b] + means the region was more democratic than the country, − less democratic.

[c] Principally, the votes for States' Rights Democrat, J. Strom Thurmond.

[d] Principally, the Alabama and Mississippi votes for slates of electors who had run unpledged and who cast their votes for Harry Flood Byrd, senator from Virginia.

[e] Principally, the votes cast for American Independent party candidate, George C. Wallace.

Further, while the South was the last region to industrialize, after 1950 it industrialized with a passion. By now it has acquired powerful new economic interests that consider the Republican party a natural home. That leaves tradition, bent and bowed, as the only one of the three major supports remaining.

The alienation of white southerners from the national Democratic party is profound. On this matter the basic electoral data are the most revealing. Table 6 shows that in 1944 the Republican national ticket was endorsed by only three southerners in ten. In 1948, when white racial protest first cut seriously into Democratic support in the region via the States' Rights candidacy of South Carolina governor J. Strom Thurmond, the Democrats still gained 52 percent of the total vote in the South, compared to 29 percent for the Republicans and 17 percent for Thurmond. In 1956, Dwight Eisenhower received a slight majority of the presidential vote from the southern states, the first Republican nominee ever to do so, but his regional percentage was well below that for the entire country.

It was not until 1960, after the civil rights movement had gathered momentum, that the GOP first achieved a higher proportion of the total vote in the South than it did in the country at large. By 1972, the South was almost as decisively Republican in presidential voting as it had once been Democratic. Richard Nixon received 59 percent of the votes in the western states and 62 percent in the Midwest. The Northeast, historically the center of Republican support, was now the most heavily Democratic, casting 42 percent of its vote for the Democratic nominee, while in the South, Nixon secured a massive 70 percent of the vote compared to 30 percent for Democrat George McGovern. These distributions are all the more striking when it is noted that black southerners, historically disenfranchised, voted in large numbers in 1972 and were overwhelmingly Democratic.

Other changes in group alignments are occurring. The New Deal coalitions were formed in a period of economic collapse and deprivation for the majority, and there have been major changes in interests and alignments as the United States has entered an "age of affluence." Organized labor, for example, which in the 1930s spoke for "have nots" and structured its electoral alliances accordingly, now represents a constituency composed essentially of marginal "haves." In general, the mixture of interests and the problems of an affluent and developed industrial society are very different from those of an earlier industrial order in the midst of economic collapse. It is hardly surprising that many of the group alignments to the parties that were nurtured in the earlier period have not survived unchanged.[21]

Any period distinguished by the erosion of long-standing group alignments to the parties, by definition a period of partisan disaggregation, must be characterized by a high level of "independent" electoral behavior. Old loyalties are breaking up, but have not disappeared. Voters find themselves cross-pressured between old ties and new interests. The sources of the collapse of old alignments manifest themselves in certain electoral contests, but not in others. Thus, in the contemporary period, white southerners have abandoned the national Democratic party en masse, but continue to express their historic loyalties by heavy Democratic voting in many state and local

[21] Ladd has discussed at length elsewhere the break up of many of the alignments which characterized the New Deal coalitions. See his *American Political Parties: Social Change and Political Response* (New York: W. W. Norton & Co., 1970), especially pp. 243-311; and Ladd, Hadley, and King, "American Party Coalitions." For a brief analysis of a similar point by Lipset, see his *Group Life in America: A Task Force Report* (New York: The American Jewish Committee, 1972); and Lipset and Carl Scheingold, "Values and Political Structure," in William J. Crotty, ed., *Assassinations and Political Order* (New York: Harper & Row, 1971), pp. 388-414.

contests. Voters leaving their ancestral party homes but not yet comfortably occupying new ones not only behave independently in the electoral arena but also describe themselves as independents—as a kind of halfway house. In 1956, according to Gallup, 15 percent of southerners described themselves as independents; eight years later it had risen to 23 percent. In 1968, 35 percent of those in the region identified as independents, a higher proportion than in any other section of the country. The percentage of independents remained extremely high in 1972, 35 percent of all voters, while 21 percent accepted the Republican, and 43 percent the Democratic label. Clearly, "independent" was a halfway house for southerners fleeing the national Democratic party.

The breakup of old group ties to the parties need not contribute to long-term partisan disaggregation. In the past, the collapse of alignments has been followed by critical realignments—that is, the establishment of new partisan identifications for significant segments of the electorate. Walter Dean Burnham, who has written the most theoretically sophisticated study of the phenomenon, describes critical realignment as involving "sharp reorganizations of the mass coalitional bases of the major parties which occur at periodic levels on the national level. . . ."[22]

In the present period, realignments surely are occurring, but it is unlikely that they will produce what the concept of a critical realignment refers to, a broad redefinition of the electoral coalitions in a new majority-minority status structure. Instead, the unraveling of the New Deal alliances seems to be producing what Samuel Lubell described as "a new alignment of two incomplete, narrow-based coalitions. . . ."[23] The key here is that party loyalties are no longer so firmly held. Realignment necessarily requires a condition of rather strong and persisting group alignments. That both the Democrats and the Republicans probably will be unable to establish decisive majority party status in national politics in the foreseeable future reflects not ineptness, or a failure to deal adequately with pressing national problems (although inadequacies there are and will surely continue to be), but the unwillingness of decisive portions of the citizenry to give the unswerving loyalty that such a coalition requires. The massive increase in formal education and the role of the electronic media—along with the more diffuse set of changes that accompany entry into a society characterized by affluence, advanced technology,

---

[22] Burnham, *Critical Elections*, p. 10.

[23] Samuel Lubell, *The Hidden Crisis in American Politics* (New York: W. W. Norton & Co., 1971), p. 278.

high physical mobility and impersonalization—have all produced an electorate which is "beyond" critical realignment, which is so fluid as to obviate the old "star and satellite" relationship.

It is a simple fact that Americans need parties much less now than in the past as intermediaries in shaping their electoral decisions. The electorate has become, for the long run, more issue oriented and more candidate oriented and, consequently, less party oriented.

In this situation, alternating landslides—achieved first by one party, then by the other—become a "natural" occurrence. Less anchored by party loyalties, more inclined to independent electoral behavior, the American electorate can be moved massively by the "events of the day," by the particular mix of candidates, programs, and problems prevailing in a given election. Massive alternations in party fortune will occur most frequently, of course, in voting for highly visible offices where candidate personality and issues become readily manifest. This weakening of party loyalties does not by itself explain why we have entered an era of "unnatural" landslides; but it does account for a context in which landslides can occur with greater ease than in the past.

Activists, Ideology, and Party Structure: A Changing Dynamic for "the Making" of the Presidential Nominee

The new political era into which the United States has entered is distinguished by the presence of new problems requiring new solutions and new collections of political interests moving toward representations not yet structured to deal with their needs. There is a sense of the inordinate rapidity of societal transformations and, in all of this, a profound awareness of intellectual groping for appropriate responses. Such historic transition periods, rare occurrences in American political history (or, for that matter, in the history of any nation), are times when "everything is up for grabs" politically. In this context, party leaders are no less confused than other segments of the society. They cannot ignore the fact that "things are changing," but they share a profound sense of uncertainty as to where it is all leading and how they should respond. Political feelings run high, but there is no widely accepted program for meeting new demands. Many of the old rules do not apply, but what are the new ones? "Conflict," not "consensus," becomes the watchword. Behind the partisan disaggregation we have been discussing is an equally profound ideological disaggregation.

The 1972 presidential election occurred in this setting—a confrontation of new problems, a juggling of new collections of interests, and this with an electorate cast adrift from its partisan moorings. Electoral instability is understandable enough. Important as this is, however, it is only part of the puzzle. For what may be the key piece, we must look to developments converging around those segments of the electorate most influential in nominating politics, especially the stratum of party activists.

One of the first attempts to locate a new dynamic in American national politics within changes affecting the activist stratum is Aaron Wildavsky's study of the Goldwater candidacy.[24] Wildavsky began by observing that "the Goldwater phenomenon is the great mystery . . . [which has] profoundly challenged accepted theories of American politics."[25] The questions Wildavsky saw being raised are essentially the same we have noted in discussing the concept of an "unnatural" landslide.

> How was it possible for a presidential nomination to go to a staunch conservative whose popularity among the electorate was known to be exceedingly low and who was far from being the preferred choice of most Republican voters? Why, in a competitive two-party system in which leaders normally seek essentially the same votes, did the parties seem to be hurtling further apart instead of coming closer together? Why, indeed, did not the minority party (the Republicans) imitate the majority party (the Democrats) in search of votes as had previously been the case? . . . To put the questions in this way suggests that we are surprised that our expectations concerning the behavior of parties and politicians have been violated. Ordinarily, we expect both major parties to choose popular candidates with a good chance of winning. The death wish is not supposed to be dominant among politicians. Party leaders are expected to conciliate groups of voters in order to get at least part of their vote.[26]

After reviewing the Goldwater phenomenon, Wildavsky concluded that it "is not a temporary aberration, but represents a profound current within the Republican party. . . ."[27]

He found the answer to the Goldwater puzzle in the emergence of a new type of activist, or more precisely the increased representa-

---

[24] Aaron Wildavsky, "The Goldwater Phenomenon: Purists, Politicians, and the Two-Party System," *Review of Politics*, vol. 27 (July 1965), pp. 386-413.

[25] Ibid., p. 386.

[26] Ibid., pp. 386-387.

[27] Ibid., p. 411.

tion in national politics of political activists with orientations different from those which we have expected in the past.

It is possible that the Goldwater phenomenon represents the beginnings of ideology in the United States. Although markedly different in their policy preferences, there are segments of the left as well as the right who are repelled by the usual patterns of democratic politics. There appears to be little difference in style between the Goldwater purists and the leftists who constantly complain about hypocrisy in public life and how the politicians sell out the people. Could it be that the United States is producing large numbers of half-educated people with college degrees who have learned that participation (passion and commitment) is good but who do not understand (or cannot stand) the normal practices of democratic politics? If this is true, we shall be hearing a great deal more from those who identify compromise with moral degeneracy. . . . For the Goldwater phenomenon which once seemed so strange, may become a persistent feature of the American political scene, nevertheless disturbing *because it reappears under different ideological guises.*[28]

Wildavsky suggested in 1965, then, that a new type of political activist might be coming into power in American presidential politics. "New" in a sense misstates the case, because antecedents of the role and its orientation can be found far earlier than the 1960s; indeed, the approach is as old as democratic politics itself. On the other hand, "new" is valid if it suggests the first emergence on the stage of American national two-party politics of a cadre of activists (whom Wildavsky labels "purists") sufficiently large to influence if not dictate the outcomes of contests for presidential nominations. Purists are a type broadly distinguished from the traditionally dominant American party activists, the "politicians."

Purists are characterized by their primary concern with issues. While wishing to win elections, they are more concerned with getting a candidate who is ideologically "right" and more sensitive to purity of program than to the maintenance of organization or to electoral victory. They are bound to the candidate by basic issue or ideological commitments. Commenting on the strength of the Goldwater movement at the grass roots level, Clifton White repeatedly stressed this issue base and emphasized its importance to the (nomination) success of the Goldwater movement. It would not be shaken by poor per-

---

[28] Ibid., p. 413. Emphasis added.

formances in primaries or in public opinion polls because victory was not the ascendant objective.[29] White wrote that

> if all his [Goldwater's] bridges went up in flames in California [the Republican primary] on Tuesday, I knew that we would have at least 550 fireproof votes surrounding and protecting him on Wednesday morning. No amount of pressure or heat would melt them away. . . . There had never been an army like this in the whole of American political warfare. . . .[30]

Wildavsky reported the same thing. He quotes one delegate respondent as saying: "The delegates are for Goldwater because they agree with his philosophy of government. That's what you people will never understand—we're committed to his whole approach."[31]

Since their political involvement started from belief in a program right and necessary, "compromise" was hardly the watchword of the Goldwater purists. Wildavsky reported the following exchange in an interview with a convention delegate:

> [Interviewer] "Do you think it's better to compromise a little to win than to lose and not compromise?"
>
> [Delegate] "I had this problem in my district. After we fighters had won [the nomination for] the congressional seat the local [Republican] machine offered to make a deal: they wouldn't oppose our candidate if we didn't oppose theirs. I refused because I didn't see how I could make a deal with the men I'd been opposing two years ago for the things they did. So I lost and I could have won easily. . . . But I don't believe that I should compromise one inch from what I believe deep down inside."[32]

Summarizing his findings, Wildavsky observed:

> Here we begin to see the distinguishing characteristics of the purists: their emphasis on internal criteria for decision, on what they believe "deep down inside"; their rejection of compromise; their lack of orientation toward winning; their stress on the style and purity of decision—integrity, consistency, adherence to internal norms.[33]

---

[29] F. Clifton White, *Suite 3505: The Story of the Draft Goldwater Movement* (New Rochelle, N. Y.: Arlington House, 1967), especially pp. 321-332.

[30] Ibid., p. 332.

[31] Wildavsky, "The Goldwater Phenomenon," p. 393. The empirical base for his observations comprised interviews with 150 delegates to the 1964 Republican Convention.

[32] Ibid., p. 395.

[33] Ibid.

The politicians, on the other hand, had a very different characteristic approach to political life: "The belief in compromise and bargaining; the sense that public policy is made in small steps rather than big leaps; the concern with conciliating the opposition and broadening public appeal; and the willingness to bend a little to capture public support are all characteristics of the traditional politician in the United States."[34]

In a study published in 1962, James Q. Wilson had developed essentially the same distinction between two sets of activists, although in a very different context. He was examining the Democratic "club movement" in New York City, California, and Illinois.[35] A sharp division had emerged among Democratic activists in these areas—one that Wilson did not then believe would move out to dominate national politics. On the one hand were the party regulars, rejected by their opponents as "hacks," "organization men," "bosses," and "machine leaders." The regulars, in turn, labeled their opposition as "dilettantes," "crackpots," "outsiders," and "hypocritical do-gooders."[36] Such tension was by no means novel: witness the long-standing struggle between "bosses" and "reformers" in urban politics. George Washington Plunkitt of Tammany Hall, a half century earlier, had seen New York reformers in essentially the same terms as had party regulars in Wilson's inquiry.[37] But as Wilson saw it, the division between the "amateur Democrat" and the "professional" had taken on a new, greatly extended dimension.

Wilson's amateur Democrat is the intellectual kin of Wildavsky's purist. He is an issue-oriented activist.

> Most generally, the amateur believes that political parties are to be programmatic, internally democratic, and largely free of a reliance on material incentives such as patronage. A programmatic party would offer a real alternative to the opposition party ["A choice, not an echo!"] A vote for the party would be as much, or more, a deliberate vote for a set of clear and specific proposals, linked by a common point of view or philosophy of government, as it would be a vote for a set of leaders.[38]

---

[34] Ibid., p. 396.

[35] James Q. Wilson, *The Amateur Democrat* (Chicago: University of Chicago Press, 1962).

[36] Ibid., p. 2.

[37] See William L. Riordon, *Plunkitt of Tammany Hall* (New York: E. P. Dutton & Co., 1963).

[38] Wilson, *The Amateur Democrat*, p. 340.

Like Wildavsky, Wilson saw the strengthening of issue activists having powerful implications for American electoral politics. Indeed separating them from the regulars are alternative conceptions of the nature of democracy generally. When the amateur Democrats were able to succeed, Wilson argued, they weakened the capacity of their party to engage in broad-based, diffuse, accommodationist, coalition-building activities.

> To the extent that the clubs can identify themselves with precise policy positions on a whole range of issues and find candidates who embody these beliefs in their manner and speech, they reduce the ability to appeal to voters on the basis of other, non-programmatic incentives, such as simple party allegiance, sectional loyalties, ethnic recognition, and personal favors. . . . If American parties have traditionally been sources of social coherence, this has in part been due to the fact that occasionally, and for very fundamental reasons, they have become identified with the opposite sides of crucial issues. . . . The amateur is . . . interested in reducing the center-seeking, consensus-building tendency of parties.[39]

Recently, Kaufman has nicely described characteristics of the issue-oriented activist stratum—although he was referring only to its left-of-center, "new politics" branch:

> The new politics is principally a politics of issues, not candidates. Loyalty to party, loyalty to candidates and winning elections are important only as they contribute to the fulfillment of the radical liberal's program and values. Those who practice the new politics are therefore ready to exercise an electoral veto on Democratic candidates when doing so serves their concern for issues. . . . The new politics implies predominant concern with the overall dynamic of the political process, not with the grubby ambitions of the lesser-evil politicians.[40]

The labels may vary but the distinction is essentially the same, whether one speaks of purists versus politicians or amateurs versus professionals. One ideal type, the issue-oriented activist, is primarily concerned with the advancement of a program. He evaluates candidates not so much as potential winners or losers, but on the basis of whether their commitments to issues are correct. The model which

---

[39] Ibid., pp. 357, 359, 360.

[40] Arnold S. Kaufman, *The Radical Liberal* (New York: Simon & Schuster, 1970), pp. xii-xiii.

he holds up for the proper functioning of a party is not one of accommodation, consensus-building, and being "all things to all people," but rather a conflict model which posits the role of parties as sharpening the divisions around crucial issues in the interest of resolving rather than papering over them. His opposite is the party-oriented activist, a role which has been dominant in American politics throughout much of our history and is intimately associated with "our expectations concerning the behavior of parties and politicians." The latter type is occupied with the maintenance of the organization and its success. It is more important that a candidate be a potential winner than that he meet closely defined issue or ideological standards. The task of party is accommodation of the broadest range of groups and interests on behalf of a majority.

Both Wildavsky and Wilson identified issue-oriented activists with a rather distinctive socioeconomic position: highly educated (in terms of formal attainment), upper-middle class, drawn heavily from professional occupations, with important leavening from the intellectual stratum. The commitment of the issue activists to their role and to their definition of the responsibilities of party are linked directly, then, to the objective characteristics of their socioeconomic position. They have the formal training necessary to participate effectively in a "politics of ideas," and their social status and economic position are such as to make unappealing or unnecessary a politics of organization maintenance and patronage.

The success of the Goldwater candidacy for the Republican nomination in 1964 appears in significant measure the product of an enormous strengthening of the position of issue activists. Goldwater was not the choice of the rank and file of the Republican politicians, such as governors, members of Congress, and other elected party officials.[41] It was, in the final analysis, a candidacy of grass roots, issue-oriented, conservative activists in the Republican party. The Arizona senator conformed superbly to the standards of this group. He carved out a distinctive, avowedly conservative program. He confronted issues directly. He made no effort to paper over differences, but rather sharpened them. He constantly displayed primary commitment to a moralistic view of politics, one which held that being "right" commended itself over trying to be "all things to all people" even if the latter course promised greater prospect for victory.

---

[41] It should be noted that Goldwater was relatively popular among one group of Republican professionals, county chairmen. A special survey of Republican county chairmen, conducted by the Gallup organization in March 1964, found the Arizona senator the first choice of nearly half the more than 1,800 chairmen who responded. *The Gallup Poll*, vol. 3, p. 1871.

Certainly Goldwater knew what was popular; he said that he knew how to play accommodationist politics if he wanted to:

> I can't help wondering, sometimes, if you have asked yourselves why my campaign is what it is. I wonder, my fellow Americans, if you think I don't *know* what views would be most popular. Do you think I don't know what Labor wants to hear, what Management wants to hear, what housewives and diplomats and white collar workers want to hear? Do you honestly think, after all these years in politics, that I don't *know* the easy way to get votes? The promises to make? The subjects to talk about—and the ones to avoid? [42]

It was the politics of morality, of ideological purity, of presenting a conflict-inviting choice rather than an accommodation-inviting echo.

The parallels in McGovern's 1972 candidacy are compelling. The South Dakota senator was not the choice of a majority of his party's rank and file. His support among the regular leadership of the party never approached majority status. But he was supported by an apparently decisive majority of issue-oriented, left-of-center activists within the Democratic party. Both friend and foe acknowledged that here was the fulcrum of McGovern's support. Thus, Michael Harrington (a friend) wrote in *The Nation* of "McGovern's basic constituency" as "issue-oriented, white, college educated." [43] And Jeane Kirkpatrick (a foe) pointed to the same issue-conscious, upper-middle class activists as the core of the movement which secured for McGovern the Democratic presidential nomination, although in terms hardly designed to be flattering:

> Intellectuals enamored with righteousness and possibility; college students, for whom perfectionism is an occupational hazard; portions of the upper classes freed from concern with economic self-interest; clergymen contemptuous of materialism; bureaucrats with expanding plans to eliminate evil; romantics derisive of *Babbitt* and *Main Street*. The values of the counterculture, spread throughout the population by expanding college enrollments, were purveyed to the public at large by magazines oriented to intellectual fashion

---

[42] A televised speech made by Senator Goldwater at Madison Square Garden in New York in the week preceding the election; as quoted by John H. Kessel, *The Goldwater Coalition: Republican Strategies in 1964* (Indianapolis, Ind.: Bobbs-Merrill Co., 1968), p. 215.

[43] Michael Harrington, "The Myth That Was Real," *The Nation*, vol. 215 (November 27, 1972), p. 521.

and by the mass media, with their elevation of the cultural category of style to paramount symbolic status.[44]

Like Goldwater's, McGovern's politics were founded on principle and moralism. "You know, all of my life I've grown up in a religious climate where I was taught that life is a struggle between good and evil, that that's what it's all about," McGovern told an interviewer.[45] The electorate, he argued, wanted a candidate who would confront issues directly, who would take clear and principled stands. "I think the American people want me to say what I believe," McGovern stated to an interviewer from a San Diego television station shortly before the California primary. "I'm not trying to get in line with Dr. Gallup. You can't straddle the issues any more." [46] The issue-oriented activists of the left, Tom Wicker observed, "had more nearly nominated an Idea—a man of courage and integrity and candor who had stumped the country for three years attacking the 'old leadership' as straddling and ducking the issues, compromising with principle, clinging to outmoded formulas and deceiving the people." [47]

There was, of course, an enormous ideological division between the activists who were decisive in the Goldwater and in the McGovern candidacies. But the similarities in many ways are more compelling. Growing numbers of issue-conscious participants have become a major force in American national politics. These activists, right and left, are dissatisfied with the accommodationist model upon which successive generations of party-oriented participants had built the familiar American two-party system. The former were not, are not, monolithic groups. The neatness of the issue-oriented or party-oriented distinction is naturally clouded in the real world of political life. What is evident is the emergence of an activist stratum, heavily college educated and middle class, inclined to substitute a conflict for an accommodation model, and preoccupied with the politics of issues and principles. No word ranks higher in the lexicon of party-directed participants than compromise. For the issue activist, by way of contrast, the country had paid a severe price for an excessive fealty to a politics of compromise.

The McGovern and Goldwater coalitions were to a notable degree bottom- rather than top-directed. They comprised movements seek-

[44] Jeane Kirkpatrick, "The Revolt of the Masses," *Commentary*, vol. 55 (February 1973), p. 61.

[45] From an interview with William Greider, reported in the *Washington Post*, October 20, 1972, p. A-16.

[46] As quoted by Tom Wicker, "McGovern With Tears," *New York Times Magazine* (November 5, 1972), p. 99.

[47] Ibid.

ing candidates, instead of being coalitions engineered by candidates. There was, of course, an important element of leadership, in that the South Dakota and Arizona senators were hardly pawns. But to a striking extent, both were cases of movements seeking spokesmen. For the Democrats, Eugene McCarthy had filled that role in 1968; in 1972, with considerably greater energy and commitment, George McGovern rode the movement to his party's nomination. It is important to see the extent to which right-of-center, issue-concerned activists on the one hand, and left-of-center activists on the other, moved by fairly clearly defined issue concerns, sought out spokesmen. Theodore White described this nicely when he referred to Goldwater as not so much the captain as "the emblem of a major *coup d'etat* in American politics." [48]

The McGovern movement in 1972 did not spring miraculously from the dissent and turmoil surrounding Vietnam. Its precursors are clearly evident, in the Democratic club movement of the 1950s and, although in a different party, the Goldwater triumph within the Republican party in 1964. For two decades, an activist stratum, split into right and left, which focuses upon the politics of issues has been gaining strength in American national politics.

The Weakening of Party Organization

The strengthening of the new activists has been aided, of course, by the weakness of regular party organization. American party structures have never been strong compared to their counterparts in Europe, and have weakened steadily in the twentieth century under repeated assaults. Most notable was the Progressive movement of the early years of this century. In their wars with the party "bosses," Progressives, in a very real sense the intellectual precursors of the Goldwater and McGovern activists of the last decade, managed to deal party organization a number of severe blows, especially in the introduction on a wide scale of the direct primary as the vehicle for nominating candidates for state and local office. Nominations would be controlled by voters who turned out in the primaries, rather than by the party organization. An issue-conscious, activist stratum, blocked by the regular party machinery, substituted a theory of intra-party democracy for one which saw democracy between the parties. The fact that for much of the United States it was an era of massive one-partyism, with Democrats dominant in the South, and

---

[48] Theodore White, *The Making of the President, 1964* (New York: Atheneum Publishers, 1965), p. 250.

the Republicans in wide areas of the North, obviously strengthened the Progressives' case. If inter-party democracy was made a sham by one-partyism, perhaps intra-party democracy was the only alternative.

In any case, the capacity of regulars to control party life was decisively weakened and a theory of intra-party democracy, compatible with the American value system with its stress on participation and egalitarianism, took root to an extent not found in any other democratic system. The widespread, casual description of party leaders able to dominate their organizations as at least slightly sinister "bosses" is indicative of the underlying legitimacy of the claim to intra-party democracy.

At the presidential level, further structural changes have weakened the always tenuous position of the regular party apparatus. Presidential preference primaries have been extended so that now twenty-three states make use of some variant of them. And after the turbulence of the 1960s had raised further questions about the capacities of regular party leadership, the Democrats' Commission on Party Structure and Delegate Selection (McGovern commission) and the reforms which it initiated carried the assault one step further. The de facto quota system for women, blacks and young people which was in force at the 1972 Democratic convention may well be removed, but a change of more fundamental importance is unlikely to be reversed. This is the requirement that delegates be selected through open processes (primaries or caucuses) at which any party member wishing to attend can do so—at the expense of the influence of party regulars.

Such formal structural changes are not the only developments weakening party organization, and particularly the role of party apparatus in the presidential nomination process. A more highly educated electorate feels less in need of organization as an active intermediary. As Moynihan has noted,

> with the educated middle class ever more involved with politics, the inclination to disdain coalition as unedifying is vastly enhanced, and as a result coalitions are collapsing everywhere. . . . For a good half century now, the concept of party reform has basically involved the weakening of party. The vocabulary of political science no less than that of political journalism reinforces this notion. Party officials are "bosses." Outsiders who want their power without their responsibility are "reformers," selfless, progressive, and, above all, democratic.[49]

[49] Daniel Patrick Moynihan, "My Turn: The Lessons of '72," *Newsweek*, November 27, 1972, p. 17.

In a climate of ever-extending egalitarianism, the established party leadership, working through such formal mechanisms as state committees and conventions, finds it increasingly hard to defend a claim to a privileged place in the determination of party affairs, and most notably on the question of who secures the party nominations.

The crumbling of party has made it easier for waves of issue activists to overwhelm the regulars and temporarily "take over" the party, imposing their preferred nominees. The ease with which the McGovern movement overwhelmed much of the regular apparatus of the Democratic party in 1972 testifies to the numbers and influence of the new activist stratum, to the immediate effects of the McGovern commission reforms, but also to the general weakness of party organization in the United States.

Conclusions

The landslides of 1964 and 1972 appear products of the emergence of a new dynamic in American national politics. In 1965, Wildavsky observed of the Goldwater-Johnson contest that "we are surprised that our expectations concerning the behavior of parties and politics have been violated." [50] Our expectations were violated in 1964, and again in 1972, because they were based on a model in which both parties rather consistently adhere to accommodationist politics.

The old dynamic seems to have been upset. The strength of party organization has continued its long-term secular decline, with the weakening intensified in the contemporary period. Issue-oriented participants in both parties, committed to a more programmatic or ideological politics, are stronger vis-à-vis the older party-oriented activists than at any earlier point in American history. The prospects for their capturing either the Republican or the Democratic nomination for President (and presumably for other major offices as well) and committing the party to a more doctrinally pure politics, with the prospect thereby of presenting a distinctly minoritarian appeal, are greater than ever before. [51]

There is no indication that rank-and-file voters are less receptive to the old accommodationist politics today than they were two decades ago. But this is not the case for important segments of the

[50] Wildavsky, "The Goldwater Phenomenon," p. 386.

[51] Lipset and Raab, "The Election and the National Mood," pp. 43-50, discuss at length the reasons why the Democratic ideological appeal proved so decisively minoritarian in 1972, a subject which we have not emphasized in the present discussion.

more active and more involved part of the citizenry parties. A situation now exists in which a major party can nominate a candidate who is the minority choice of the rank and file, considered "too extreme" by many, and hence who submits to a massive defeat even in the absence of that mix of candidate personal attributes and valence issues which have in the past been associated with landslides. Furthermore, this situation appears to have been elevated to the position of a "natural" occurrence. It follows readily enough under the new dynamic.

What, then, for the future of American presidential politics? Lubell's prediction, made in 1970, of "a new [partisan] alignment of two incomplete, narrow-based coalitions, polarized against each other," seems valid. With party identification greatly weakened for a growing segment of the electorate, with independent voting a more frequent occurrence, and with the increasing likelihood of major party candidates perceived as ideologically "extreme," there is a prospect of massive, alternating landslides.

There is a distinct possibility, of course, that in a given election both parties might nominate candidates seen by large segments of the electorate to be "away from the center." In such instances, low levels of electoral turnout, a diminished sense of the legitimacy of the outcome, and frequent sorties by third party candidates can follow as readily as a massive victory by one of the major party contenders.

As long as the United States operates with a "one-man" executive (in contrast to the cabinet type) and with a "winner-take-all" electoral system (the electoral college), prospects for a regularized multi-party system appear dim. Much more likely is the continuance of a greatly weakened but still ostensibly two-party system, characterized by frequent reversals of massive proportions and nothing approaching a stable presidential majority. With dominant activists more programmatically concerned and less in sympathy with a politics of accommodation, the prospects are also high that the majority of the electorate will find itself confronting presidential contests in which the stakes appear greater than they have typically seemed to be in the past.

We hold no apocalyptic visions for the future of American politics. It appears, simply, that elections like 1972 will be not uncommon occurrences in the future. The most striking feature, and the lasting importance, of the "unnatural" contest between Richard Nixon and George McGovern is not that McGovern lost and lost badly; not just that a large segment of the electorate found itself unimpressed by both candidates and wound up either not voting or choosing with reservations; and not only that a "New Politics" wing of the Democratic party came of age and succeeded in imposing its choice. It is, rather, that a dynamic is now at work which makes such occurrences "natural."

The only way an electorate can leave its mark upon the policy process is by saying yes or no to the alternatives presented to it. For this reason, an era of negative landslides carries serious consequences for democratic decision making. Large numbers of voters feel deprived of a satisfactory choice. Big majorities are produced, but these are in no sense mandates. A lack of competitiveness and the general atmosphere of negativism reduce the incentive to participate and render campaigns a far less meaningful medium for policy debate. Ultimately demoralized oppositions are unable to test the victors effectively. No group in the population, whatever its politics, can escape these consequences. College faculty, along with the rest of the American electorate, found themselves in 1972, as in 1964, engaged in a presidential contest poorly suited to test the adequacy or inadequacy of the preceding four years of decision making.

3
FACULTY ELECTORAL BEHAVIOR IN 1972

The several disparate currents thus far discussed—the disproportion- ately left-of-center orientation of college professors vis-à-vis most strata in the population, the presence of sharp and stable political divisions within the faculty, the weakened, and hence fluid character of party loyalties, especially among highly educated Americans, and the predominantly negative cast of much of the voting in the 1972 presidential election, reflecting unenthusiasm with the choices pre- sented—are all evident in the electoral behavior of the professoriate in the Nixon-McGovern contest. In tying together these various strands, it is appropriate to begin with the basic voting patterns among academics. We know what kind of a year 1972 was for Republicans nationally, but what did it prove to be within the major group of the intellectual community, the professoriate? How did faculty vote distributions compare to those of the general public and of other population subgroups, both in absolute terms and with reference to the "swing" from the preceding election? Was 1972 a year of Republican success or unsuccess in the universities?

Faculty Voting in 1972: The Basic Results

As noted in the preface, our information on the voting behavior and various political opinions of professors in 1972 came from a national telephone survey (with 472 respondents) which we conducted be- tween August 29 and September 13, 1972, and from a post-election follow-up survey with the same respondents, administered by mail.[1]

---

[1] While standard sampling procedures were observed and confidence in the reliability of the findings must be based there upon, it is nonetheless informative to note the close parallels between distributions located by the small 1972 survey

Table 7
FACULTY PRESIDENTIAL VOTE PREFERENCES, 1972
(all data presented as row percentages)

	McGovern	Nixon	Other	Undecided
1972 vote intent (September), with those undecided included	48	45	1	6
1972 vote intent (September), with the "undecideds" excluded from the computations	51	48	1	—
1972 vote (post-election survey)	56	43	1	—

Table 7 shows that McGovern and Nixon were running a virtual dead heat among professors in early September. The Democratic nominee enjoyed, according to the survey, a scanty three percentage point lead over his Republican opponent. But there was a modest shift toward McGovern between September and election day, one of about 5 percent. Thus, Senator McGovern, backed by just under 38 percent of the national electorate and loser to Richard Nixon by a margin of 23 percentage points, was supported by 56 percent of the academics and carried this group by a 13 point margin.

Universities were widely perceived to be islands of Democratic strength in a Republican presidential sea in 1972. Clearly, there is

and those revealed by the exhaustive study (60,000 respondents, one-third of the entire professoriate) conducted under the sponsorship of the Carnegie Commission on Higher Education three years earlier. In all cases where such comparisons are possible, they show the highest consistency. For example, professors were asked both in the 1969 and 1972 surveys how they had voted in 1968:

	Humphrey	Nixon	Wallace	Other
1969 Survey	58	39	—	4
1972 Survey	56	40	—	4

Similarly, respondents in both studies were invited to locate their political views on a five point scale, from "left" to "strongly conservative," and again the variations are insignificant.

	Left	Liberal	Middle-of-the-road	Moderately conservative	Strongly conservative
1969 Survey	5	40	27	25	3
1972 Survey	9	40	26	23	2

In objective personal characteristics—such as age, religious background, and academic discipline—the distributions contained in our recent survey match closely those known to exist among the faculty at large.

ample basis for this view. McGovern's support in the professoriate was about 18 points higher than in the general public. Other surveys have shown a similarly high (if not what some had anticipated) performance by the Democratic nominee among college students.[2] Further analysis is necessary, however, to round out our evaluation of the strength or weakness of the 1972 Republican presidential showing among academics. For one thing, we need to compare the partisan distribution of professorial ballots in 1972 to that in earlier presidential contests.

A number of studies give some indication of the electoral behavior of college professors in past presidential elections. But only three comprised national samples of the entire professoriate. These were a survey conducted by Lawrence C. Howard in 1956, which yields data on faculty voting in 1948, 1952 and 1956,[3] the big 1969 Carnegie faculty survey, with voting data for the 1964 and 1968 presidential elections, and our own 1972 study. The data base for temporal comparisons is therefore scanty, and the problem is further compounded by acknowledged weaknesses of one of the three surveys. Howard did not provide adequate documentation on his 1956 investigation, and received only a 35 percent return of the mailed questionnaires.[4] His own assessment—that "the results . . . are not thought to be mathematically precise . . ." but provide a general indication of distributions in faculty voting—seems justified.[5] Nevertheless Howard's survey provides the only existing data on electoral behavior by academics in 1948, 1952 and 1956 (although Paul Lazarsfeld and Wagner Thielens, Jr. conducted a rigorous survey of social scientists, which includes data on their electoral preferences in 1948 and 1952).[6]

With these qualifications, Table 8 offers some basis for general observation of Nixon's electoral performance among faculty voters compared to that of earlier Republican candidates. The 43 percent of the vote which he received was about the highest of any Republican presidential candidate in the last three decades. Eisenhower's 1952 showing was probably comparable. Dewey in 1948, Eisenhower in 1956, Goldwater in 1964, and Nixon himself in 1968 all received

---

[2] An election day survey by CBS News found 54 percent of students between 18 and 24 years of age voting for McGovern, 45 percent for Nixon, with 1 percent for minor party candidates. "Preliminary Tabulations, CBS News Election Day Survey," mimeographed (New York: CBS News, 1972).

[3] Lawrence C. Howard, "The Academic and the Ballot," *School and Society*, vol. 86 (November 22, 1958), pp. 415-419.

[4] Ibid., p. 416.

[5] Ibid.

[6] Lazarsfeld and Thielens, *The Academic Mind*. See Chapter 1 of this volume.

Table 8

PRESIDENTIAL VOTE OF FACULTY AND GENERAL PUBLIC, 1948-1972

(all data presented as row percentages)

	Faculty			National Electorate		Percentage Margin Between Faculty Vote and National Vote	
	Democratic	Third party	Republican	Republican	Democratic	Republican	Democratic
1948[a]	50	11	39	45	50	− 6	0
1952[a]	54	2	44	55	44	−11	+10
1956[a]	60	2	38	57	42	−19	+18
1960[b]	—	—	—	—	—	—	—
1964[c]	77	1	22	39	61	−17	+16
1968[c]	58	4	39	43	43	− 4	+15
1972[d]	56	1	43	61	39	−18	+17

[a] A national survey of faculty, conducted by Lawrence C. Howard in 1956. Number of respondents—1284. Lawrence C. Howard, "The Academic and the Ballot," *School and Society*, vol. 86 (November 22, 1958), pp. 415-19.

[b] No national survey.

[c] Carnegie faculty survey, 1969; number of respondents—60,028.

[d] Ladd-Lipset faculty survey, 1972; number of respondents—472.

a smaller percentage of faculty votes. Nixon appears to have improved modestly upon his 1968 showing, a result somewhat more impressive than it might seem at first glance because the gain came without benefit of a Wallace electorate to absorb. While George Wallace picked up 13.5 percent of the total popular vote in 1968, he was backed by just 1 percent of professors. Wallace's absence from the 1972 contest, working to Nixon's advantage in the general public, was not at all a factor in the President's performance among academics. However, the main conclusion one draws from Table 8 is that faculty electoral distributions have borne a notably consistent relationship to the national vote. Professors gave Stevenson a proportion of their vote 18 percentage points higher than he received from the entire electorate; McGovern's faculty total exceeded his nationwide percentage by 17 points. Professors have been much more supportive of Democratic and, especially in 1948, left third party candidates than have voters generally, and no significant change has occurred over the past seven elections. Nixon's 1972 vote from faculty is entirely consistent with the performance of previous Republican candidates. He improved upon Goldwater's share of faculty ballots by 21 points, while building upon the 1964 Republican nominee's proportion of the total vote by 22 points.

Table 9 examines the Republican professorial vote from another perspective, comparing the 1968-1972 "swing" of academics to that of other groups in the population. The Republican vote nationally increased by 17.4 percentage points from 1968 to 1972. In contrast, the swing to the Grand Old Party among professors was only four percentage points—smaller than for any other group in the population which we have been able to identify. It is interesting to note in Table 9 that the increase in the Republican presidential vote from 1968 to 1972 was the smallest in upper socioeconomic status groups (the college educated, persons in professional and managerial occupations) and much larger for groups of lower socioeconomic status (manual workers, those with a grade-school or high-school education). The Republican gain for persons with a college education and under 35 years of age—seven percentage points—was very close to the swing among professors.

These data say something, of course, about the location of relative strength and weaknesses in McGovern's appeal. For a Democratic nominee, he ran unusually poorly among low-status whites, while doing relatively well among the college educated and other high socioeconomic status groups, especially among the college-educated young. For example, while McGovern lost by a significantly larger margin in 1972 than did Stevenson in 1956, his vote among the college educated was six points higher (37 percent support as against 31 percent) than Stevenson's had been sixteen years earlier.

Table 9

REPUBLICAN GAINS IN PRESIDENTIAL VOTE, FACULTY AND OTHER POPULATION STRATA, 1968–1972 [a]

(all data presented as row percentages)

	1968 Republican Presidential Vote	1972 Republican Presidential Vote	Republican Swing 1968—1972
FACULTY	39	43	+ 4
ALL VOTERS	43.4	60.8	+17.4
Education			
College	54	63	+ 9
Under 35 years of age	43	50	+ 7
35-49	56	65	+ 9
50 years and older	63	73	+10
Noncollege	40	61	+21
Under 35 years of age	38	60	+22
35-49	39	62	+23
50 years and older	44	62	+18
High school	43	66	+23
Grade school	33	51	+18
Occupation			
Professional and managerial	56	69	+13
Clerical and sales	47	64	+17
Manual	35	57	+22
Religion			
Protestants	49	70	+21
Catholics	33	52	+19
Jews	10	29	+19
Race			
Blacks	10	17	+ 7
Whites	47	68	+21
Age			
Under 30 years of age	38	52	+14
30-39	43	63	+20
40-49	46	62	+16
50 years and older	47	64	+17

[a] Data on population subgroups are from the *Gallup Opinion Index,* Report No. 90 (December 1972), p. 10; or have been computed from "raw" Gallup data. In the latter case, two surveys were combined for each election year, to increase the *n* upon which percentages are based. For 1968, AIPO Surveys #770 and #771; for 1972, AIPO Surveys #859 and #860.

The data in Table 9 also show the effects of Wallace's candidacy in 1968 and of his absence from the contest in 1972. One of the reasons the pro-Republican swing was so small within the professoriate, as compared with the general public, was the absence of any Wallace support to be absorbed. We see something of this same factor, although at a much less significant level, for high socioeconomic status groups generally. Since about two-thirds of the 1968 Wallace voters backed Nixon in 1972, the fact that only 9 percent of the college educated—as contrasted to 15 percent of the noncollege —had been Wallace adherents obviously means that there was less potential for a Republican swing among them.

While McGovern's overall electoral performance among university voters was a relatively strong one, there were signs of weakness even on the surface. He ran behind Democratic candidates for Congress, although not by nearly so large a margin as he did in the electorate at large. Sixty-one percent of professors cast their ballots for Democratic congressional candidates, as compared to the 56 percent support McGovern received. Nixon was the choice of 43 percent of professors voting in the presidential election, but Republican congressional candidates received just 37 percent of faculty ballots. A liberal, antiwar Democratic presidential nominee, who relied heavily upon a base of support in colleges and universities, in fact ran less well among professors than did his party's congressional candidates.

We discussed in Chapter 2 the big increase during the past decade in the proportion of the electorate describing themselves as independents and engaging in independent electoral behavior, especially among those who have had formal higher education. Apart from the matter of how professorial votes were distributed in 1972, the extraordinary weakness of party ties and loyalties stands out as a notable finding of our survey. Gallup studies in 1972 showed independents to be the largest "party" among college-educated Americans, a status they hold even more emphatically in the professoriate. Half of the faculty (49 percent) described themselves as independents, while 37 percent identified as Democrats, and just 13 percent as Republicans. The picture developed in Chapter 1 of the professoriate distinguished by a tendency to view politics in ideological or issue-oriented terms is dramatically reinforced here. Faculty members are disproportionately liberal or left of center in their political views, and as such disproportionately Democratic. Their consistently high support for Democratic nominees seems less a product of strong party loyalties than of issue commitments.

As Table 10 demonstrates, only 30 percent of our faculty sample both identified themselves as Democrats and voted for McGovern in 1972, while 12 percent of all respondents were Republican identifiers voting for Nixon. Thus, about three professors in five (58 percent) failed to meet what must be considered a minimal test of party regularity: profession of an identification with the party and support for its presidential nominee in a single election. Even more striking, perhaps, is the fact that only one-fourth (26 percent) of Nixon's faculty support came from self-described Republicans, while Democrats provided 17 percent and independents an extraordinary 57 percent of the total. McGovern, on the other hand, drew more heavily upon party identifiers, but even he received only half (52 percent) of his votes from self-identified Democrats, with another 4 percent coming from Republicans and 44 percent from independents. Twenty percent of the Democratic identifiers "defected" to vote for Nixon, while 14 percent of Republicans backed the Democratic presidential nominee. Independents split evenly, 50 percent for each of the major party contenders. In short, a growing tendency toward independent electoral behavior, noteworthy among groups of high socioeconomic status generally, is especially striking in the faculty.

Before we turn to examine the sources of Nixon's and McGovern's support among faculty, what conclusions can we draw about the overall success or the lack thereof of the major parties

Table 10

FACULTY PARTY IDENTIFICATION AND PARTY VOTING, 1972

Party Identification	McGovern Voters	Nixon Voters
"Grand Total" Percentages[a]		
Democratic	30	7
Republican	2	12
Independent	25	25
Row Percentages[b]		
Democratic	80	20
Republican	14	86
Independent	50	50
Column Percentages[c]		
Democratic	52	17
Republican	4	26
Independent	44	57

[a] Each cell n divided by the total n.

[b] Democratic, $n = 173$; Republican, $n = 59$; Independent, $n = 229$.

[c] McGovern voters, $n = 238$; Nixon voters, $n = 184$.

in the 1972 elections? There are grounds for describing the election as a relatively successful one for McGovern within the universities, and conversely for Nixon. The Democratic nominee, so badly beaten in the national vote, won a solid majority among professors. And his faculty vote surpassed his national proportion by a margin (17 points) almost identical to that achieved by Democratic nominees over the past two decades. On the other hand, running as a liberal and antiwar nominee (in university circles, where liberal and antiwar sentiments were predominant), with his candidacy heavily reliant upon university support, and contesting a Republican who has never been the darling of American intellectuals, McGovern gained a smaller proportion of the faculty vote in 1972 than did Democratic congressional candidates. Nixon's academic vote in 1972 was as high as any achieved by a Republican presidential nominee apparently since the New Deal and, at 43 percent of the total, constitutes a solid if minority position. Thus the presidential election as contested in the colleges and universities produced something of a mixed result. There was no Democratic erosion comparable to that in the public at large or among most population subgroups, but neither was there an especially strong McGovern performance, as might have been expected in view of the long-standing university commitment to liberal candidates and programs. For more definite conclusions, we must begin to untangle the sources of Nixon's and McGovern's support in universities, and how faculty saw the points at issue in this contest.

Faculty Voting in 1972: A Case of Familiar Internal Differentiation

In previous analysis of survey data on college and university professors taken primarily from the 1969 Carnegie survey, we have identified a set of variables which are associated with especially sharp differences in faculty political orientations.[7] The discipline in which the faculty member teaches, the type of school in which he is located, along with other measures of his scholarly or intellectual achievement, and his age are linked causally to large, systematic differences in faculty orientations across a broad range of social and political questions—both intramural and affecting the larger society. Support for Nixon and McGovern strongly reflects these basic underlying patterns in political commitments. Thus, the Democratic nominee was backed by three-fourths of faculty in the liberal social sciences,

---

[7] Earlier publications of ours discussing this are cited in Note 1 of the Preface. For a brief discussion of some of these relationships in the present volume, see Chapter 1, pp. 27-32.

by seven in ten among humanists, by just half of the natural scientists, and by only 30 percent of professors in the conservative, business-related applied fields (engineering, business administration, departments of colleges of agriculture). Differences in voting patterns between professors in the social sciences and those in the business applied fields vastly exceeded those separating such grossly differentiated groups in the larger society as businessmen and manual workers, or the young and the old. While in one sense such comparison is specious, it is interesting to note that the margin in McGovern support between social scientists and engineers in the academic world (approximately 50 percentage points) was about as great as that between blacks and whites in the society at large.

Younger faculty have consistently been more liberal with respect to both societal and campus issues than their older colleagues. The existence of this "generation gap" within the professoriate must be seen both as a result of the general processes which moderate views as people grow older and take on a variety of family and career responsibilities, and as a consequence of the special characteristics of the university. Inherent in the relationship between scholarship and iconoclastic views is the constant introduction into universities of young people who are highly responsive to the rebellious currents characteristic of their time.[8]

Strong as the relationship is between age and political commitments, it is not uniform across the entire range of issues. The gap between young and old faculty on questions of student protests and demonstrations in the late 1960s was greater than in matters of civil rights policy for the larger society. The reason here is straightforward enough. The student protests were much more directly an age-related issue. Young professors as a group were simply closer in interests, perspectives and status to the protesting students than were their senior colleagues. In some elections, variations in vote distribution among the several age groups of the faculty have been large, in others minimal. Support for Henry Wallace, the Progressive party candidate for President in 1948, was much higher among young than older faculty. Lazarsfeld and Thielens found, for example, that 17 percent of social scientists thirty years of age and younger backed Wallace or Socialist Norman Thomas, compared to just 3 percent of

[8] We have discussed the effect of aging upon political views elsewhere. See by Lipset and Ladd, "College Generations—From the 1930's to the 1960's," *The Public Interest*, vol. 25 (Fall 1971), pp. 99-113; and in expanded format, "The Political Future of Activist Generations," in Philip G. Altbach and Robert S. Laufer, eds., *The New Pilgrim: Youth Protest in Transition* (New York: David McKay Co., 1972), pp. 63-84.

the professors in the social sciences who were sixty years and older.[9] In 1964, on the other hand, age-related differences in professorial voting were nonexistent (Table 11). Goldwater was deemed unacceptable by an overwhelming majority of faculty in all age brackets.

Not surprisingly, there was high correlation between age and presidential choice in 1972, one much greater than in the electorate as a whole. Seventy-one percent of professors under thirty-five backed McGovern, as against only 42 percent of their colleagues over fifty years of age. In the electorate at large, according to Gallup survey data, 42 percent of voters under thirty-five backed the Democratic nominee, compared to 36 percent in the fifty and over group, a margin of just 6 percent.

We discussed in Chapter 1 reasons why the more eminent faculty have shown a greater proclivity for left-critical politics than their less highly achieving colleagues. This same relationship is evident in 1972 presidential voting. McGovern was the choice of more than 70 percent of faculty at institutions of high academic standing, but was supported by less than half of professors at lower-tier schools.[10] Noteworthy in the 1972 results, however, is a partial exception to the frequent finding in faculty studies of a strong relationship between intellectual accomplishment and political views. Looking at respondents in terms of personal accomplishments—for example, publication record over the last two years—we find McGovern weakest among those with no publications (43 percent support) and strongest among faculty with a moderate record of scholarly attainment (66 percent McGovern backers). Surprisingly, the Democratic nominee's strength dropped off considerably among the most highly productive scholars—54 percent support among those who had published five or more items over the past twenty-four months. The reasons for this are most appropriately discussed in the following chapter. It is enough to note here that it stands as an exception to the general rule of McGovern's strength increasing with the scholarly standing of the faculty.

Table 11 points up the fact that the falling off of Democratic presidential support (1972 compared to 1968) occurred disproportion-

---

[9] Data from the Lazarsfeld-Thielens study (*The Academic Mind*) were made available to us by the Bureau of Applied Social Research, Columbia University.

[10] As indicated in the note to Table 11, all colleges and universities in both the 1969 Carnegie study, and in our own 1972 survey, were classified according to a three-item index of academic standing. Clearly, "upper tier" and "lower tier" fail to do justice to the variety in the scholarly standing of American colleges and universities. But given the size of our 1972 sample, no finer classification scheme was justified.

Table 11

FACULTY PRESIDENTIAL VOTING, BY SELECTED PERSONAL AND PROFESSIONAL CHARACTERISTICS

(all data presented as row percentages)

	1972[a]			1968[b]				1964[b]		
	Dem.	Rep.	Other	Dem.	Rep.	A.I.P.	Other	Dem.	Rep.	Other
Age										
Under 35	71	29	c	60	35	1	4	77	22	1
35-49	60	40	c	60	37	1	2	79	21	1
50 years and older	42	58	c	53	44	2	1	76	23	1
Religious Background										
Jewish	88	9	2	87	8	c	6	97	2	1
Catholic	54	46	c	68	27	2	3	81	18	1
Protestant	51	49	c	52	45	1	2	74	26	1
Field										
Social sciences	76	22	2	75	20	c	5	89	10	2
Humanities	71	29	c	72	23	1	4	86	13	1
Natural sciences	53	47	c	57	40	2	2	77	22	1
Business-related applied fields	30	70	c	38	58	3	1	62	37	c
Publications										
Five or more	54	44	1	65	31	1	3	84	15	1
One to four	66	34	c	62	35	1	2	81	18	1
None	43	57	c	54	42	2	2	74	26	1
School Quality[d]										
Upper tier	72	27	1	71	26	c	3	87	12	1
Lower tier	46	54	c	59	38	2	2	78	22	1

[a] Ladd-Lipset faculty survey, 1972.　　[b] Carnegie faculty survey, 1969.　　[c] Less than one percent.

[d] All colleges and universities in both the 1969 and 1972 survey were ranked by a three-item index of academic standing. We have described the construction of this index in note 45 of Chapter 1. "Upper tier" includes index scores of 3-9; "lower tier," scores 13-18.

ately at the lesser rather than the better colleges and universities. Indeed, all of the *net* decline was accounted for by faculty at the former places. The pronounced liberalism characteristic of elite institutions seems to be the decisive element in the above pattern. Currents producing a major Democratic defection nationally in 1972 were bound to be much more influential in schools where the prevailing ideological—and hence partisan—balance was relatively even than where it was heavily tilted one way. The massive liberal and Democratic ascendancy at elite centers sustained an environment which discouraged defections to the Republicans. The country moved Republican in 1972, and many individual voters experienced interpersonal relations which encouraged them to move in this direction. No such pattern took shape in the heavily Democratic upper reaches of American higher education.

For the most part, we have found that the political views of faculty are little affected by their socioeconomic backgrounds. When professors are arrayed according to class origins, for example, there are no significant political differences. Whether the faculty member was brought up in a working-class family of parents who had not completed the twelfth grade or was the child of a university-trained professional is of little importance to his or her present political opinions. Neither parental occupation nor parental education is significantly correlated with any political opinion variable in our surveys. Apparently, the long and intense socialization process which produces the requisite training for a career in higher education generally supersedes any impact of background on present politics. Religious origins, however, are another matter. Faculty members of Protestant and Catholic parentage do not, as groups, differ much in their politics but, as we have demonstrated in other publications, Jewish faculty are much more liberal-left than their Gentile associates. This is evident in presidential voting.[11] Thus, in 1964 Johnson was the choice of 97 percent of Jewish faculty, compared to 74 percent of Protestants. In 1972, McGovern received the electoral support of approximately 90 percent of academics of Jewish background, in contrast to just over 50 percent among those of Protestant and Catholic parentage.

As Milton Himmelfarb has pointed out, Jews among the public at large voted more heavily Democratic in 1972, as in 1968 and earlier, "than any other body of white voters—Protestants, Catholics, businessmen, farmers, workers; even professors; even students."[12]

[11] Lipset and Ladd, "Jewish Academics in the United States," "The Divided Professoriate," and "The Politics of American Political Scientists."

[12] Milton Himmelfarb, "The Jewish Vote (Again)," *Commentary*, vol. 55 (June 1973), p. 81.

But the increase in Republican support between 1964 and 1972 was considerably greater for Jews generally (19 percent) than for Jewish academics (7 percent). Here is yet another indication of the importance of immediate social milieu for electoral decision making. The country swung massively from the Democrats in 1972, but academe did not. Especially at elite colleges and universities, where Jewish faculty are heavily represented, Republican voting remained, in the face of the Nixon landslide, the "deviant" case. Informal processes of social contact and interaction continued to reinforce the tendency to vote Democratic in the many liberal enclaves of American higher education.

The American professoriate is hardly of one cloth. Although as a group its members are disproportionately inclined to liberal causes and manifested this by being one of the few identifiable population groups to give majoritarian support to the Democratic presidential nominee in 1972, there are a variety of distinct subcultures in the university world. A social scientist from an elite college or university moved socially with colleagues who supported McGovern over Nixon by an overwhelming margin. On the other hand, professors in engineering or business administration, especially at schools of the middle or lower range, were moving in an environment equally Republican. Those outside the university are often unappreciative of the range in political orientations subsumed by its several subcultures. It is especially important to note that the difference in the proportion of Nixon support from young social scientists at elite institutions to older professional school faculty at middle- to lower-tier schools was greater than that between almost any other two identifiable strata in the electorate.

Faculty Voting, 1968 and 1972: What Shifts Occurred?

The modest gains in faculty votes made by the Republicans in 1972, compared with 1968, occurred in the face of a strong countercurrent which brought McGovern significant support that Humphrey had lost four years earlier. Table 12 shows that a full fifth of 1972 McGovern supporters either backed third parties in 1968 (exclusively third parties of the left) or sat out the election even though they were eligible to vote. In sharp contrast, Nixon received only 8 percent of his total faculty vote from those who either sat out the earlier presidential contest or cast ballots for a third party candidate. Among professors who did not vote in the Humphrey-Nixon contest but

Table 12

COMPARISON OF FACULTY VOTING, 1968 AND 1972
(all data as percentages of *n*)

1968 Vote	Presidential Vote in 1972, by 1968 Vote			
	McGovern	Nixon	Other[a]	Nonvoters
Humphrey (*n* = 219)	78	17	1	5
Nixon (*n* = 155)	14	83	1	3
Other[a] (*n* = 15)	87	6	6	—
Nonvoters (*n* = 72)	44	18	1	36

1972 Vote	Presidential Vote in 1968, by 1972 Vote			
	Humphrey	Nixon	Other[a]	Nonvoters
McGovern (*n* = 236)	72	9	6	14
Nixon (*n* = 181)	20	71	1	7
Other[a] (*n* = 5)[b]	—	—	—	—
Nonvoters (*n* = 40)	25	10	—	65

[a] Exclusively for minor parties of the left.

[b] *n* is too small.

did go to the polls in 1972, McGovern outdistanced Nixon by a margin of more than seven to three.

On the other hand, Nixon succeeded in 1972 in dislodging a substantial number of Humphrey adherents. Nearly a fifth of the academics who voted Democratic in 1968 supported Nixon four years later. And a full fifth of Nixon's faculty backers in 1972 had been in Humphrey's camp in the preceding election. By way of contrast, just 9 percent of McGovern's voters had favored Nixon in the 1968 balloting.

Two main currents are evident, then, in faculty presidential voting in 1972. One consists of 1968 nonvoters and third party "defectors" enlisting as McGovern supporters by an overwhelming margin. The other, slightly stronger numerically, consists of Humphrey voters switching over to the Republican nominee whom they had rejected in the preceding election.

Thus far, some of the structural properties of the 1972 vote in universities have been located but little has been said about the source of the patterns, especially of the shifts from 1968. That subject, involving the ideological or issue base of the 1972 vote, occupies us in the following chapter.

4

McGOVERN AND NIXON VOTERS: THE IDEOLOGICAL BASE OF THE 1972 VOTE

Ideology influences the electoral behavior of college and university professors to an unusually high degree. In other words, choice among competing candidates reflects, much more than in the general public, systematically arrayed sets of orientations along a wide range of issues. An ideology can be thought of as a patchwork quilt, with individual policy items as the patches. Like such a quilt, an ideology is more than the sum of its patches; it is the patches bound together in a specified and ordered way. A person sees politics in ideological terms when he applies some "abstract and far-reaching conceptual dimension" to sort out and put in order a wide range of disparate policy questions, when he binds together a collection of policy "patches" to form a programmatic "quilt." The general tendency of professors as "men of ideas" to see political life ideologically is evident in their attitudes toward electoral affairs.

It comes as no surprise, then, to find Nixon and McGovern voters among the professoriate far more sharply and systematically differentiated in their policy preferences than the larger bodies of adherents of the Republican and Democratic nominees in the general public. The issue distance between McGovern and Nixon adherents in the professoriate is extraordinarily large.

Ideological Profiles of Nixon and McGovern Voters

No issue of national or international affairs has occupied American academics as completely since 1965 as America's involvement in Vietnam. Professors have been seen, and rightly, as a principal source of opposition to U.S. policies in the Indochina war and, along with their student apprentices, as the very fulcrum of protest and dissent. The visibility of academic protests on the war has sometimes, however, served to obscure the existence of significant, if minority, support for Nixon administration policies. The 1969 Carnegie survey found about three-fifths of all faculty then favoring an immediate unilateral U.S. withdrawal from Vietnam, or an immediate reduction of American involvement coupled with encouragement of a coalition government in South Vietnam to include the Viet Cong. At the same time, however, a substantial minority supported what later came to be known as Vietnamization: "to reduce . . . [American] involvement, while being sure to prevent a Communist takeover in the South." And 8 percent of professors in 1969 actually endorsed a position more "hard line" than that of the administration, arguing that "the United States should commit whatever forces are necessary to defeat the Communists."

By the time of our 1972 survey, the dimensions of the Vietnam issue had changed somewhat. Desire to see the United States extricated immediately had spread much more widely through the population. But there was a sharp division over how American extrication should be achieved, a division rather neatly presented in the positions taken by the two 1972 presidential candidates. We asked our faculty respondents: "Which of these positions on Vietnam is closer to your own: That the United States should unilaterally withdraw from Vietnam at once; or that the United States should continue with the present 'Vietnamization' program?" The former alternative, clearly, was McGovern's, the latter Nixon's. A decisive majority (57 percent) of the faculty supported immediate withdrawal, but a strong minority (34 percent) favored Vietnamization, while 9 percent felt that their preferences were not adequately subsumed by either alternative.

The position of professors on whether the unfolding of the Vietnamization program had been basically sound or unsound was associated to an exceptionally high degree with their preference for Nixon or McGovern. Thus, 87 percent of faculty who favored immediate unilateral withdrawal voted for the Democratic candidate, while the same proportion exactly (87 percent) who endorsed Vietnamization voted Republican. Table 13 shows that just 8 percent of McGovern voters supported Vietnamization, and only 16 percent of Nixon's backers were in favor of immediate and unilateral United States withdrawal from Vietnam.

In 1968, when Hubert Humphrey secured 58 percent of faculty ballots, a significant minority of those who opposed him appeared to do so because of his identification with the Johnson war policies.

Table 13

FACULTY POSITIONS ON VIETNAM, BY PRESIDENTIAL VOTE CHOICE

(all data presented as percentages of *n*)

	Withdrawal	Vietnamization	Dissatisfaction with Either Approach as Presented
All McGovern voters (*n* = 219)	86	8	7
All Nixon voters (*n* = 155)	16	70	14
Switchers, Humphrey in 1968, Nixon in 1972 (*n* = 37)	32	42	26
Switchers, Nixon in 1968, McGovern in 1972 (*n* = 21)	85	10	5
All third party voters and nonvoters in 1968 (*n* = 67)	69	24	7
Third party voters and nonvoters in 1968, McGovern in 1972 (*n* = 45)	90	5	5

More than 2 percent voted for leftist third party candidates, men like Dick Gregory and Eldridge Cleaver, who are not even on the ballot in most states. More significantly, a proportion of Richard Nixon's 1968 vote came from professors who thought of themselves as liberals and who were strongly antiwar. The 1969 Carnegie survey showed more than 7 percent of Nixon backers in favor of an immediate, unilateral United States withdrawal from Vietnam, while 9 percent described their political views as "left" or "liberal." They presumably saw their Nixon votes as a protest against the Democratic party establishment, or identified Nixon as more likely to end the war than Johnson's vice president. There is also evidence that a considerable segment of the 11 percent of faculty who did not vote in 1968 were liberals withholding their support from the Democratic nominee because of antiwar feelings. Thus, a higher proportion of nonvoters in 1968 (29 percent) than of Humphrey adherents (22 percent) favored, in the spring of 1969, an immediate unilateral withdrawal from Southeast Asia.

Table 13 shows that faculty voting for Nixon in 1968 but for McGovern in 1972 were overwhelmingly antiwar and in favor of a unilateral United States withdrawal. From answers to open-ended questions in the survey, we are able to detect two principal groups among the Nixon-to-McGovern switchers. In one camp are faculty who voted Republican in 1968 purely as a means of protesting Democratic war policies. A philosopher at a leading private university, for example, said that he had "voted for Nixon four years earlier on the theory that you should vote the bastards out of office." McGovern was taking a position on the war which he favored, and naturally enough he was returning to the Democratic fold. The second group, in contrast, believed that Nixon really would extricate the United States from Vietnam quickly, and went against him in 1972 because he had not. We also see from the data in Table 13 that about two-thirds of all faculty who voted for third party candidates in 1972 or who sat the election out were, in 1972, proponents of a unilateral U.S. withdrawal from Vietnam. Those who came to support McGovern—a large majority of the third party voters and the eligible nonvoters of four years earlier—were even more overwhelmingly antiwar than the rank and file of McGovern adherents. McGovern drew support from three groups who had not been Democratic in 1968—a segment of Nixon voters, third party voters, and nonvoters—all of whom were strong opponents of American Vietnam policy and who had been dissatisfied with Humphrey's candidacy mainly on the grounds of his association with the war.

On the other hand, faculty who had supported Humphrey in 1968 but shifted to Nixon seemed to have switched less directly as a result of the war policies or proposed programs of the 1972 contenders. Some did endorse Vietnamization, but this group was a much smaller proportion than among all Nixon voters. An unusually high percentage (26 percent) expressed reservations with both the withdrawal and the Vietnamization alternatives. His position on the war, so influential in bringing faculty support to McGovern, appears much less linked to the substantial erosion which he experienced among a category of Humphrey backers.

Nixon and McGovern adherents in the professoriate are very sharply differentiated in self-descriptions of their political philosophies. Nearly 80 percent of those who voted for McGovern described their political views as left or liberal, in striking contrast to just 13 percent of Nixon backers. A majority of all faculty who voted for Nixon in 1972 identified themselves as conservatives, a label not especially in vogue in universities, and one accepted by

Table 14

FACULTY POLITICAL SELF-DESCRIPTION, BY PRESIDENTIAL VOTE CHOICE
(all data presented as row percentages)

	Left-Liberal	Middle-of-the-Road	Conservative
All McGovern voters	78	17	6
All Nixon voters	13	36	52
Switchers, Humphrey in 1968, Nixon in 1972	25	53	22
Switchers, Nixon in 1968, McGovern in 1972	42	26	32
All third party voters and nonvoters in 1968	76	20	5
Third party voters and nonvoters in 1968, McGovern in 1972	58	27	15

only a quarter of the professoriate. Professors switching from Nixon to McGovern (1968 and 1972 votes) as a group are considerably more liberal than those who stayed with Nixon, but considerably less liberal than the rank and file of McGovern's faculty supporters. Faculty who backed Humphrey in 1968 but switched to Nixon four years later paint a distinctive collective self-portrait of themselves as middle-of-the-roaders. As would be expected, professors who voted for third party candidates in 1968 or sat the election out, and then went on to support McGovern in 1972, see themselves disproportionately as left of center; only 5 percent in this group are self-described conservatives.

In earlier analyses of faculty political orientations, we have noted a strong link between general ideology, as reflected in views on national and international questions, and positions on a variety of campus controversies—such as the protests and demonstrations of the late 1960s, preferential hiring or admissions policies for underrepresented groups, more "student power" (that is, a broader voice by students in university decision making), and the like.[1] The source of the high correlations between general liberalism-conservatism and positions on many campus issues is in one sense obvious enough. Commitment

---

[1] See especially "American Social Scientists and the Growth of Campus Political Activism in the 1960's," "The Politics of American Political Scientists," "The Politics of American Sociologists," and "Politics of Academic Natural Scientists and Engineers."

to egalitarian and popular causes in the larger society has its counter-
part in a more egalitarian and popular posture on strictly intramural
controversies. The extent of the correlation across an array of super-
ficially disparate items again testifies to the highly constrained or
ideological character of the thinking of a large proportion of the
faculty. Strong as the overall association is, however, it should be
pointed out that significant numbers of academics who are national
liberals strongly opposed protests and demonstrations and the new
politicization of academic affairs, on grounds that such developments
posed a threat to academic freedom and to a university committed to
scholarly excellence.

We find (Table 15) an especially strong correlation between
support for Nixon and opposition to the increase of campus activism
in the late 1960s and early 1970s. Respondents to our 1972 survey
were fairly evenly divided in their overall assessments of the student
protests: 38 percent indicated general approval, 48 percent disapproval, with 14 percent displaying conflicting assessments. A full
80 percent of those in the approval category voted for McGovern,
while 70 percent who described their position as one of disapproval
backed Nixon. Just one quarter of McGovern's voters among the
faculty indicated opposition to student activism, compared to nearly
three-fourths of Nixon voters.

The hypothesis was offered at the outset that campus protests,
but more generally the whole politicization of universities in recent
years, had led to the emergence of new divisions among professors
which would manifest themselves in the 1972 presidential voting. It
was postulated that Senator McGovern, in part because activist students and young faculty furnished the core of his most visible
supporters in many university communities, would find the faculty
response to his candidacy significantly affected by these new internecine divisions and, in particular, that he would experience some
attrition of support among normally Democratic professors who had
reacted negatively to the activism of recent years and of its attendant
manifestations. Table 15 provides some tentatively confirming data
on this. Whereas just 26 percent of those voting for McGovern
expressed general opposition to student activism, 60 percent of
professors who had been for Humphrey in 1968 but switched to
Nixon in the 1972 balloting expressed such opposition. The Hum-
phrey-to-Nixon switchers, similarly, contained a notably high proportion who were against assigning "a large share of future faculty
vacancies" to groups such as blacks and women which have been
underrepresented, who rejected the proposition that "the recent

Table 15

FACULTY POSITIONS ON CAMPUS POLITICAL ISSUES, BY PRESIDENTIAL VOTE CHOICE

(all data presented as row percentages)

	Opposed to Student Activism [a]	Opposed to Preferential Hiring for Underrepresented Groups [b]	Opposed to Faculty Unionism [c]	Opposed to Faculties Taking Collective Stands on Major Controversies [d]
All McGovern voters	26	43	34	58
All Nixon voters	73	61	59	67
Switchers, Humphrey in 1968, Nixon in 1972	60	60	58	67
Switchers, Nixon in 1968, McGovern in 1972	25	50	40	52
All third party voters and nonvoters in 1968	35	46	36	60
Third party voters and nonvoters in 1968, McGovern in 1972	17	46	37	58

a "What has been your general position on the emergence of radical student activism in recent years, approval or disapproval?"

b "Do you agree or disagree . . . that groups which are underrepresented on the faculty—such as blacks, Chicanos and women—should be assigned a large share of future faculty vacancies until they are proportionately represented?"

c "Do you agree or disagree . . . that the recent growth of unionization of college and university faculty is beneficial and should be extended?"

d "Do you agree or disagree . . . that it is desirable for college and university faculty to put themselves on record by vote on major political controversies?"

growth of unionization of college and university faculty is beneficial and should be extended," and who disagreed that "it is desirable for . . . faculty to put themselves on record by vote on major political controversies." McGovern's relative weakness among senior faculty of high scholarly attainment, noted in Chapter 3, seems a product of this group's disproportionate opposition to aspects of the "new academic politics" and their association of the Democratic nominee with it.

Although it is hard to be precise on the matter, we also find in our data some indication that events of the last half decade or so may have contributed to the creation of a conservative attitude of a special sort among a segment of the professoriate. It is a special variety because it is not manifested in conventional policy areas such as support for civil rights and civil liberties, backing for social welfare measures, and adherence, in general, to programs commonly thought of as liberal. It involves something more nearly akin to the Burkean than to the post-New Deal concept of conservatism. The social turbulence of recent years appears to have impressed upon a portion of the faculty a greater sense of the fragility of societal institutions, more appreciation of unintended, negative consequences of change, a feeling for the importance of civil order. This surely does not indicate a swing to the right in the American professoriate, but rather a change in conceptual orientation that touches strains historically associated with conservatism.

The ideological sources of Nixon's and McGovern's support, and of vote switching between the 1968 and 1972 presidential elections, are evident enough. McGovern drew his backing from left-to-liberal faculty, traditionally Democratic, and he significantly increased Humphrey's 1968 base by bringing left and antiwar professors back to the party fold. At the same time, he lost ground as about a fifth of academics who backed Humphrey over Nixon in 1968 switched to Nixon's camp in 1972. Table 16, along with data already presented, brings out the most salient ideological characteristics of the switchers. Academics who describe their politics as left or liberal gave Nixon almost exactly the same proportion of their vote (just over 10 percent) in each election. Similarly, conservatives were overwhelmingly Republican in both 1968 and 1972. A major shift occurred, however, among self-described "centrists." A decisive majority voted for Humphrey over Nixon in 1968; but by a margin of more than six to four this group backed Nixon over McGovern four years later. McGovern also lost significant support among Humphrey voters of four years earlier who resented campus protests and politicization.

Table 16 shows, for example, that professors indicating opposition to student activism divided fairly evenly between Nixon and Humphrey in 1968, but voted overwhelmingly Republican in 1972. In general, McGovern lost support exactly where he would have been expected to have lost it, in view of his policies and the base upon which his candidacy was built: among middle-of-the-road Democrats and independents, including especially, it seems, those hostile to the "new academic politics" of the preceding half decade.

The Choice in 1972: As Professors Saw It

Thus far, the bases of Nixon's and McGovern's support in universities have been described in terms of personal and professional characteristics and of ideological orientations. It is possible to take our analysis one step further and examine the specific reasons which our respondents themselves offered in explaining their vote choice. All faculty interviewed in the 1972 study were asked: "In assessing your vote, what consideration(s) do you find of paramount importance? What, more than anything else, led you to make the choice you did?" Answers were unusually elaborate and precise, and together with

Table 16

1972 AND 1968 VOTE OF PROFESSORS, BY POLITICAL SELF-DESCRIPTION AND POSITION ON STUDENT ACTIVISM

(all data presented as row percentages)

	1972			1968		
	McGovern	Nixon	Other	Humphrey	Nixon	Other
Political self-description						
Left or liberal	88	12	1	82	11	7
Middle-of-the-road	37	62	1	54	45	1
Conservative	12	88	—	13	86	1
Position on student activism						
Approval	79	20	1	71	20	9
Uncertain; conflicting assessments	74	26	—	69	31	—
Disapproval	31	69	—	43	56	1

responses to related questions, provide a rather comprehensive picture of the considerations most salient to our faculty sample.

We noted in Chapter 2 that a prime factor in a contest like the 1972 presidential election is a high level of voter apathy and general negativism. The dynamic of the new landslides is such that a significant segment of the electorate feels dissatisfied with the choice it is being asked to make, and winds up either not voting or choosing reluctantly. This negativism pervades faculty assessments of the 1972 presidential contest and indeed is the predominant response. Reading through the nearly 500 interviews, one is more than struck by the "anti" character of the 1972 vote—one is almost overwhelmed by it.

Distrust of Nixon and dissatisfaction with his Vietnam and domestic policies comprised McGovern's greatest boons among academics. Over and over again, McGovern's backers cited things wrong with the Republican incumbent as their prime reason for voting Democratic. A professor of civil engineering at a southern university described his vote for McGovern as simply due to "a lack of a suitable alternative." Long-standing "Nixonphobia" was frequently cited. Said a political scientist at a small eastern college: "I have always found voting against Nixon one of my easiest tasks." As a professor of English at a southwestern university put it, "I continue to regard Nixon as a threat to national sanity." Again: "I have voted against Nixon for years and did so again with enthusiasm. I dislike and distrust him intensely. Mine was a vote of 'no confidence' in the incumbent."

Other McGovern voters were more specific in their criticisms of Nixon. Even in November the issue of corruption was often raised. "The issues of integrity in government and credibility—rather the lack of it," said a professor of classics. "Mr. Nixon has never deigned to comment on the charges of sabotage and espionage. No public official should feel he is above accountability." Interestingly enough, however, in view of developments to come, not a single respondent in our faculty survey referred specifically to Watergate. The relatively low saliency of the affair in late 1972, evident for the population at large, held as well for the professoriate. Many McGovern electors took issue with the record of the Nixon administration in the area of civil liberties. A professor of physics at a West Coast university asserted: "Constitutional rights are incompatible with Nixon." A psychologist at a southern university cited "Nixon's erosion of freedom of speech, and his selection of Supreme Court justices." Yet another McGovern voter, a molecular biologist, explained his choice this way: "Domestic issues; Nixon is no friend of the conservationists or the consumerists. His record on curbing inflation is awful." The comments of a professor of law at an East Coast institution captured the flavor of the comments of many faculty who voted for McGovern as they tried to explain their decision: "Nixon represented a greater evil and was surrounded by more dangerous men; McGovern's inabilities might have led to equally awful results, but at least his heart was more or less right. I wish there was a 'no vote' that would prompt new elections."

On the other hand, a large segment of Nixon's voters stressed dissatisfaction with McGovern as the prime reason for their choice. "Radicalism" and a general feeling that the South Dakota Democrat was not "up to the job" were the criticisms most commonly offered. For example:

McGovern is not up to the job; also, he is too radical.

I don't think McGovern could effectively take care of the problems of the Presidency. Also, he is too indecisive. He is okay as a Senator from South Dakota, but not as President.

My vote was one against McGovern's indecision, his style and his lack of integrity.

McGovern did not impress me as being responsible or capable.

Both candidates, of course, had ardent admirers. Faculty members who voted for McGovern and who offered positive reasons for doing so most often cited what they felt was the courage and correctness of his position on Vietnam. Nixon admirers, on the other hand, most frequently used the word "competent." A biological scientist at a midwestern university spoke of his confidence in the President's "ability to lead the country effectively." A west coast chemist said he voted for Nixon because of "the feeling that Nixon would be vastly more competent and decisive in dealing with the array of national and international problems." On more specific, substantive matters, the President received high marks from a number of his supporters for accomplishments in the area of foreign relations.

The explanations which our faculty respondents gave for their presidential choices in 1972 have been categorized in a number of different ways. Table 17 represents an effort to organize these many and disparate responses into four basic groups which together account for about 80 percent of all of the individual evaluations. The first contains explanations of the decisive factor, which focus upon positive attributes—personal and programmatic—of the favored candidate. The second comprises assessments stressing failures or inadequacies

Table 17

PRINCIPAL DETERMINANTS OF FACULTY
1972 PRESIDENTIAL VOTE
(all data presented as row percentages [a])

	Favorable References to the Preferred Candidate	Unfavorable References to the Major Alternative	Gross Dissatis-faction with Both Candidates; But a Choice Must be Made	Positions on the War in Vietnam
All McGovern voters	13	14	17	34
All Nixon voters	30	27	8	15
Switchers, Humphrey in 1968, Nixon in 1972	18	27	23	18
Switchers, Nixon in 1968, McGovern in 1972	19	10	14	43
Third party voters and nonvoters in 1968, McGovern in 1972	19	8	11	49

[a] Row percentages do not equal 100 because various miscellaneous responses have not been included.

of the only viable alternative. The third group bears some resemblance to the second but differs in its emphasis upon basic dissatisfaction with both major party candidates: "a plague on both your houses." Faculty in this category wound up voting, but with a distinct lack of enthusiasm. Finally, there is a group of responses focusing upon the war in Vietnam. Some of these could have been grouped into categories one or two, since they involve both criticism and praise of Nixon and McGovern positions. But the war was such a prime determinant of the vote of so large a segment of the professoriate that it seemed desirable to include together all vote explanations which raised the war as the decisive consideration.

A full third of McGovern's faculty adherents cited the war in Vietnam as the main determinant of their voting decision. An even higher proportion (43 percent) of faculty who voted for Nixon in 1968 but switched to McGovern in the past election gave war-related matters this primacy. And a full half (49 percent) of professors who backed third party candidates or were nonvoters in 1968 and moved to McGovern's camp in 1972 said that matters related to the war were decisive in their electoral choice.

Nixon voters were influenced much more, Table 17 shows, by general reactions, favorable and unfavorable, to the two candidates. Thirty percent of Nixon's backers cited accomplishments or positive attributes of the Republican incumbent as determining their choice, whereas only 13 percent of McGovern's supporters offered favorable assessments of the South Dakota Democrat as the primary reason for their decision. An almost equally high proportion (27 percent) of Nixon's adherents said that negative attributes of the Democratic nominee were decisive. The fact that a much higher share of Nixon's than of McGovern's backers gave positive or conversely negative candidate references of a general nature as the primary reasons for their vote has three main sources: (1) that Nixon, as the incumbent President, had a concrete record, notably his attainments in foreign policy, for his proponents to applaud; (2) that McGovern suffered a special loss of confidence in his abilities to handle the presidency; and (3) most importantly, the fact that McGovern's position as an antiwar candidate loomed so large in his overall profile. Much of the support for the Democrat's position on Vietnam was coupled, of course, with negative assessments of administration policies.

Overall, Table 17 confirms the highly negative character of faculty voting in 1972. The dynamic leading to this "unnatural landslide" produced much the same effect, then, among professors as among the general public. The election was marked by absence of enthusiasm in a substantial sector of the professoriate. Especially striking is the underlying weakness of McGovern's appeal, in view of his position as a liberal, antiwar candidate who relied so heavily upon an activist stratum in the university.

Brief reference should be made to that 5 percent of our sample who indicated in early September an intention to vote Republican but wound up shifting to the Democratic nominee. These campaign switchers display a remarkably uniform profile. They are moderate liberals or centrists who voted for Humphrey in 1968 and who had serious reservations about both of the 1972 major party candidates. Their shift to McGovern as the campaign progressed seems rooted in the negativism we have been describing. They were finally drawn to the Democratic camp less by the positive appeals of McGovern's candidacy than as an act of voters with serious dissatisfactions concerning the choice before them "returning to the fold." These intra-campaign switchers were strongly cross-pressured. Their normal inclination was to vote Democratic, but they had reservations about the 1972 Democratic nominee. A decisive factor in their decision to return to the fold seems to have been the environment in which they moved. Ninety percent of this small group were at "elite" schools whose faculties, as we have noted, were heavily for McGovern.

There may appear to be, on the surface, a contradiction between our earlier emphasis on the impact of new campus divisions upon McGovern's candidacy and the failure of any significant segment of the professoriate to cite this factor in explaining their vote. While we have no data which deal conclusively with this, we doubt that there is in fact any inconsistency. It is more likely that a segment of the professoriate whose opposition to the "new campus politics" led them to an aversion to McGovern—whom they associated with this politics—chose not to engage in so involved an explanation of their presidential assessments, even if they were conscious of it, and instead expressed concern about McGovern's "competency" for the job of President.

Conclusions

On university campuses, the 1972 election was both "business as usual" and something quite new, reflecting currents in the larger society. As to the first, Nixon and McGovern drew heavily upon traditional Republican and Democratic bases of support in the professoriate, and the disproportionate liberalism of the faculty, compared to the public at large, resulted in an academic vote for the Democratic nominee far in excess of what he achieved in the entire electorate. On the other hand, McGovern's candidacy did not, ultimately, strike a strongly responsive chord in the universities—even though he had, of course, his strong partisans, as did Nixon.

In one sense, 1972 was a story of opportunities missed for the Republican party. University faculty had not swung to the right in any general ideological sense, but there had been a notable reaction to the "new campus politicization" of the late sixties and early seventies which redounded to McGovern's disadvantage. Probably no other matter, as we noted in Chapter 1, had ever so divided the American university, severing social and intellectual relations, as the controversies over how to deal with student protest.

On almost every campus which faced a major crisis—for example, Berkeley, Columbia, Cornell, Harvard, and San Francisco State—the faculty split, sometimes formally, into two or three major factions or faculty political parties. These groups usually operated with elected executive committees, prepared strategies for dealing with faculty committees, and the like. The parties have been variously described as right, center, and left; as hard, compromise inclined, and soft; as hawks, temporizers, and doves.

This pattern has been discussed by John Spiegel, whose Lemberg Center for the Study of Violence had been engaged in analyses of specific campus conflicts. He has identified the three faculty positions by

> (1) a desire to support the goals of the aggrieved students while minimizing any loss of face to the institution for what may be interpreted as surrender. This position is usually called the "soft line" advocated by the "doves"; (2) a desire to defeat and punish the students while minimizing any loss of face to the institution for what may be interpreted as callousness or cruelty. This policy is the "hard line" pursued by the "hawks"; (3) a middle ground, or temporizing position, which attempts to placate both the "hawks" and the "doves," in part, while also partially satisfying the demands of the students—a balancing act which requires great skill, diplomacy, flexibility and inventiveness, plus some Machiavellian sleights of hand.
>
> . . . The "hawks" can scarcely conceal their contempt for the "doves"—those "bleeding hearts," those "masochists" who, perhaps unconsciously, are out to wreck the university. On their side, the "doves" show a mild but persistent abhorrence of the wrath, and in their eyes, "sadism" of the "hawks." Privately, they tend to believe, for the moment at least, that most of the "hawks" are paranoid personalities.
>
> . . . The "temporizers" had been impressed by the amount of movement shown by the school prior to the initial disorder. They had shared vicariously or actually, the "liberalization" of American life in recent decades. . . . Accordingly, they feel offended by the ingratitude of the aggrieved students, who, in their perception, are "biting the hand that feeds them." [2]

Similar divisions with explicit factions emerged in many of the national professional associations such as the American Political Science Association, the Modern Language Association, and the American Anthropological Association. Their conventions and elections of officers reflected the deep ideological divisions within their member-

---

[2] John P. Spiegel, "The Group Psychology of Campus Disorders: A Transactional Approach," mimeographed (Waltham, Mass.: Lemberg Center for the Study of Violence, Brandeis University), pp. 13, 17.

ships. Recurrent issues were the propriety of academic groups passing political resolutions, particularly bearing on the Vietnam War,
and the appropriateness of faculty undertaking government-supported
policy research.

Professors also divided over proposals to modify the traditional
academic commitment to meritocratic standards. Many opposed efforts to establish quotas for groups—such as blacks, Chicanos, and
women—underrepresented on faculties and in student bodies.

Data from our two national surveys, and from a number of more
localized studies as well, indicate that the divisions among faculty
were linked to general ideological orientations. The more leftist faculty tended to back student activism and favor official political action
by professorial groups, while their more conservative colleagues
opposed these positions. More interesting, however, is the fact that
significant numbers of academics of liberal persuasion took the "conservative" or "moderate" position in the intramural debates. To a
notable degree, the latter were older, often quite prestigious, individ-
uals, heavily involved in research activities. For them, keeping the
university a meritocratic "house of study" was a crucial matter.

Since many prominent figures associated with the antiwar "New
Politics," such as Senators McGovern and Fulbright, backed the line
of argument presented by the left faculty caucuses, we anticipated,
as noted earlier, that the internecine cleavage would affect national
political attitudes and behavior of more moderate professors, including their voting decisions. In fact, however, the effects which can be
detected in the 1972 elections are limited.

In a sense, therefore, 1972 was a story of opportunities missed
by the Republican party. The reasons for the failure are manifold.
But to a considerable extent, we believe, the GOP was unable to
take advantage of the divisions within the university because many
of its leaders failed to differentiate among professors. Higher education was, simply, enemy territory. Some politicians in both parties
exploited popular concern about campus protests, but Republicans
were typically in the forefront. Ronald Reagan, for example, was
elected governor of California in 1966 campaigning on the Berkeley
issue. In speeches before and after taking office, he blamed the
faculty as a group both for not spending enough time with students
and for not taking sanctions against student demonstrators. Various
speeches by President Nixon and Vice President Agnew were inter-
preted as blanket attacks on faculty and administrators.

Republicans can argue, and rightly, that their party was in fact
divided, and that some of its leaders have championed university

interests. In view of the antipathy of faculty for the Republicans, however, a concerted effort by the minority party to win academic support was required. Instead, the *prevailing* Republican tone was one of suspicion, if not outright hostility.

It is not surprising, then, that in spite of the identification of George McGovern with student activism and support of the counter-culture, a climate of distrust of Republicans continued, particularly in the predominantly liberal, upper-tier universities. Coupled with the long-standing Democratic ascendancy among academics, this produced a situation of minimal Republican gains among faculty (and, probably, intellectuals generally) even when the party's presidential nominee was carrying the country so heavily.

The most striking feature of the 1972 presidential election among academics remains the lack of enthusiasm for both candidates, reflecting the reaction in much of the national electorate and attributable in large measure to the same dynamic. Despite the lopsided nature of the final results, American voters did not bestow an overwhelming mandate. Nor, for many of the same reasons, did the professoriate.